Geoffrey Chaucer's

The General Prologue to the Canterbury Tales

MODERN CRITICAL INTERPRETATIONS

Geoffrey Chaucer's

The General Prologue to the Canterbury Tales

Edited and with an Introduction by

Harold Bloom

Viva Books

New Delhi | Mumbai | Chennai | Kolkata | Bengaluru | Hyderabad | Kochi | Guwahati

First Indian Edition 2007
Reprinted 2011

VIVA BOOKS PRIVATE LIMITED

- 4737/23 Ansari Road, Daryaganj, New Delhi 110 002
  E-mail: vivadelhi@vivagroupindia.net, Tel. 42242200
- 76, Service Industries, Shirvane, Sector 1, Nerul, Navi Mumbai 400 706
  E-mail: vivamumbai@vivagroupindia.net, Tel. 27721273, 27721274
- Jamals Fazal Chambers, 26 Greams Road, Chennai 600 006
  E-mail: vivachennai@vivagroupindia.net, Tel. 28290304, 28294241
- B-103, Jindal Towers, 21/1A/3 Darga Road, Kolkata 700 017
  E-mail: vivakolkata@vivagroupindia.net, Tel. 22836381, 22816713
- 7, Sovereign Park Apartments, 56-58, K. R. Road, Basavanagudi, Bengaluru 560 004
  E-mail: vivabangalore@vivagroupindia.net, Tel. 26607409, 26607410
- 101-102 Mughal Marc Aptt., 3-4-637 to 641, Narayanguda, Hyderabad 500 029
  E-mail: vivahyderabad@vivagroupindia.net, Tel. 27564481, 27564482
- First Floor, Beevi Towers, SRM Road, Kaloor, Kochi 682 018, Kerala
  E-mail: vivakochi@vivagroupindia.net, Tel: 0484-2403055, 2403056
- 232, GNB Road, Beside UCO Bank, Silpukhuri, Guwahati 781 003
  E-mail: vivaguwahati@vivagroupindia.net, Tel: 0361-2666386

Published by arrangement with:

Facts on File, Inc.
132 West 31st Street
New York NY 10001
USA

ISBN : 978-81-309-1874-7

Published by Vinod Vasishtha for Viva Books Private Limited, 4737/23, Ansari Road, Daryaganj New Delhi - 110 002. Printed and bound by Anand Sons, Delhi - 110 092.

Contents

Editor's Note

This book gathers together a representative selection of the best modern critical interpretations of the General Prologue to the *Canterbury Tales* of Geoffrey Chaucer. The critical essays are reprinted here in the chronological order of their original publication. I am grateful to Bruce Covey for his erudition and judgment in helping me to edit this volume.

My introduction meditates upon Chaucer's originality in the representation of human character, and is greatly influenced by the work of the late E. Talbot Donaldson, the effect of which can be measured in several of the essays in this book. Ruth Nevo begins the chronological sequence of criticism with her study of the ordering of the pilgrims, in terms of their acquisition and use of wealth.

In Jill Mann's essay, the emphasis is upon satiric imagery, while the late Donald R. Howard's discussion centers upon the role of memory in Chaucer's tale-telling and character portraiture. Loy D. Martin explores the relation between typology and characterization, after which Jane Chance establishes the role of the Genesis account of the Creation in Chaucer's General Prologue.

Geoffrey Hughes intimates some of the relations between linguistic and social change in the *Canterbury Tales,* while H. Marshall Leicester, Jr., investigates problems of voicing and representation in Chaucer's great work. The shape of the poem is illuminated by the late Morton W. Bloomfield's account of narrative frameworks, after which Patricia J. Eberle returns us to Ruth Nevo's subject, the worldly and financial status of the pilgrims.

In this book's final essay, Barbara Nolan takes us back to the concern of Talbot Donaldson and of Leicester with Chaucer's voices, and usefully divides the Prologue into the various tonalities that Chaucer so vivaciously rendered.

Introduction

I

Chaucer is one of those great writers who defeat almost all criticism, an attribute he shares with Shakespeare, Cervantes, and Tolstoy. There are writers of similar magnitude—Dante, Milton, Wordsworth, Proust—who provoke inspired commentary (amidst much more that is humdrum) but Chaucer, like his few peers, has such mimetic force that the critic is disarmed, and so is left either with nothing or with everything still to do. Much criticism devoted to Chaucer is merely historical, or even theological, as though Chaucer ought to be read as a supreme version of medieval Christianity. But I myself am not a Chaucer scholar, and so I write this introduction and edit this volume only as a general critic of literature and as a common reader of Chaucer.

Together with Shakespeare and a handful of the greater novelists in English, Chaucer carries the language further into unthinkable triumphs of the representation of reality than ought to be possible. The Pardoner and the Wife of Bath, like Hamlet and Falstaff, call into question nearly every mode of criticism that is now fashionable. What sense does it make to speak of the Pardoner or the Wife of Bath as being only a structure of tropes, or to say that any tale they tell has suspended its referential aspect almost entirely? The most Chaucerian and best of all Chaucer critics, E. Talbot Donaldson, remarks of the General Prologue to the *Canterbury Tales* that:

> The extraordinary quality of the portraits is their vitality, the illusion that each gives the reader that the character being described is not a fiction but a person, so that it seems as if the poet has not created but merely recorded.

As a critical remark, this is the indispensable starting-point for reading Chaucer, but contemporary modes of interpretation deny that such an illusion of vitality has any value. Last June, I walked through a park in Frankfurt, West Germany, with a good friend who is a leading French theorist of interpretation. I had been in Frankfurt to lecture on Freud; my friend had just arrived to give a talk on Joyce's *Ulysses*. As we walked, I remarked that Joyce's Leopold Bloom seemed to me the most sympathetic and affectionate person I had encountered in any fiction. My friend, annoyed and perplexed, replied that Poldy was *not* a person and that my statement therefore was devoid of sense. Though not agreeing, I reflected silently that the difference between my friend and myself could not be reconciled by anything I could say. To him, *Ulysses* was not even persuasive rhetoric, but was a system of tropes. To me, it was above all else the personality of Poldy. My friend's deconstructionism, I again realized, was only another formalism, a very tough-minded and skeptical formalism. But all critical formalism reaches its limits rather quickly when fictions are strong enough. L. C. Knights famously insisted that Lady Macbeth's children were as meaningless a critical issue as the girlhood of Shakespeare's heroines, a view in which Knights followed E. E. Stoll who, whether he knew it or not, followed E. A. Poe. To Knights, Falstaff "is not a man, but a choric commentary." The paradox, though, is that this "choric commentary" is more vital than we are, which teaches us that Falstaff is neither trope nor commentary, but a representation of what a human being *might* be, if that person were even wittier than Oscar Wilde, and even more turbulently high-spirited than Zero Mostel. Falstaff, Poldy, the Wife of Bath: these are what Shelley called "forms more real than living man."

Immensely original authors (and they are not many) seem to have no precursors, and so seem to be children without parents. Shakespeare is the overwhelming instance, since he swallowed up his immediate precursor Christopher Marlowe, whereas Chaucer charmingly claims fictive authorities while being immensely indebted to actual French and Italian writers and to Boccaccio in particular. Yet it may be that Chaucer is as much Shakespeare's great original as he was Spenser's. What is virtually without precedent in Shakespeare is that his characters *change themselves by pondering upon what they themselves say*. In Homer and the Bible and Dante, we do not find sea-changes in particular persons brought about by those persons' own language, that is, by the differences that individual diction and tone make as speech produces further speech. But the Pardoner and the Wife of Bath are well along the mimetic way that leads to Hamlet and Falstaff. What they say to others, and to themselves, partly reflects what they already are, but partly engenders also what they will be. And perhaps even more subtly and forcefully, Chaucer suggests ineluctable transformations going on in the Pardoner and the Wife of Bath through the effect of the language of the tales they choose to tell.

Something of this shared power in Chaucer and Shakespeare accounts for the failures of criticism to apprehend them, particularly when criticism is formalist, or too given over to the study of codes, conventions, and what is now called "language" but might more aptly be called applied linguistics, or even psycholinguistics. A critic addicted to what is now called the "priority of language over meaning" will not be much given to searching for meaning in persons, real or imagined. But persons, at once real *and* imagined, are the fundamental basis of the experiential art of Chaucer and Shakespeare. Chaucer and Shakespeare know, beyond knowing, the labyrinthine ways in which the individual self is always a picnic of selves. "The poets were there before me," Freud remarked, and perhaps Nietzsche ought to have remarked the same.

II

Talbot Donaldson rightly insists, against the patristic exegetes, that Chaucer was primarily a comic writer. This need never be qualified, if we also judge the Shakespeare of the two parts of *Henry IV* to be an essentially comic writer, as well as Fielding, Dickens, and Joyce. "Comic writer" here means something very comprehensive, with the kind of "comedy" involved being more in the mode, say, of Balzac than that of Dante, deeply as Chaucer was indebted to Dante notwithstanding. If the Pardoner is fundamentally a comic figure, why, then, so is Vautrin. Balzac's hallucinatory "realism," a cosmos in which every janitor is a genius, as Baudelaire remarked, has its affinities with the charged vitalism of Chaucer's fictive world. The most illuminating exegete of the General Prologue to the *Canterbury Tales* remains William Blake, whose affinities with Chaucer were profound. This is the Blake classed by Yeats, in *A Vision,* with Rabelais and Aretino; Blake as an heroic vitalist whose motto was "Exuberance is Beauty," which is an apt Chaucerian slogan also. I will grant that the Pardoner's is a negative exuberance, and yet Blake's remarks show us that the Wife of Bath's exuberance has its negative aspects also.

Comic writing so large and so profound hardly seems to admit a rule for literary criticism. Confronted by the Wife of Bath or Falstaff or the suprahumane Poldy, how shall the critic conceive her or his enterprise? What is there left to be done? I grimace to think of the Wife of Bath and Falstaff deconstructed, or of having their life-augmenting contradictions subjected to a Marxist critique. The Wife of Bath and difference (or even differance")? Falstaff and surplus value? Poldy and the dogma that there s nothing outside the text? Hamlet and Lacan's Mirror Phase? The heroic, he vitalizing pathos of a fully human vision, brought about through a upermimesis not of essential nature, but of human possibility, demands a riticism more commensurate with its scope and its color. It is a matter of esthetic tact, certainly, but as Oscar Wilde taught us, that makes it truly a moral matter as well. What devitalizes the Wife of Bath, or Falstaff, or Poldy, tends at last to reduce us also.

III

That a tradition of major poetry goes from Chaucer to Spenser and Milton and on through them to Blake and Wordsworth, Shelley and Keats, Browning and Tennyson and Whitman, Yeats and Stevens, D. H. Lawrence and Hart Crane, is now widely accepted as a critical truth. The myth of a Metaphysical counter-tradition, from Donne and Marvell through Dryden, Pope, and Byron on to Hopkins, Eliot, and Pound, has been dispelled and seen as the Eliotic invention it truly was. Shakespeare is too large for any tradition, and so is Chaucer. One can wonder if even the greatest novelists in the language—Richardson, Austen, George Eliot, Dickens, Henry James, and the Mark Twain of *Huckleberry Finn* (the one true rival of *Moby-Dick* and *Leaves of Grass* as *the* American book or Bible), or Conrad, Lawrence, and Faulkner in this century—can approach Shakespeare and Chaucer in the astonishing art of somehow creating fictions that are more human than we generally are. Criticism, perhaps permanently ruined by Aristotle's formalism, has had little hope of even accurately describing this art. Aristophanes, Plato, and Longinus are apter models for a criticism more adequate to Chaucer and to Shakespeare. Attacking Euripides, Aristophanes, as it were, attacks Chaucer and Shakespeare in a true prolepsis, and Plato's war against Homer, his attack upon mimesis, prophesies an unwaged war upon Chaucer and Shakespeare. Homer and Euripides, after all, simply are not the mimetic scandal that is constituted by Chaucer and Shakespeare; the *inwardness* of the Pardoner and Hamlet is of a different order from that of Achilles and Medea. Freud himself does not catch up to Chaucer and Shakespeare; he gets as far as Montaigne and Rousseau, which indeed is a long journey into the interior. But the Pardoner *is* the interior and even Iago, even Goneril and Regan, Cornwall and Edmund, do not give us a fiercer sense of intolerable resonance on the way down and out. Donaldson subtly observes that "it is the Pardoner's particular tragedy that, except in church, every one can see through him at a glance." The profound phrase here is "except in church." What happens to, or better yet, *within* the Pardoner when he preaches in church? Is that not parallel to asking what happens within the dying Edmund when he murmurs, "Yet Edmund was beloved," and thus somehow is moved to make his belated, futile attempt to save Cordelia and Lear? Are there any critical codes or methods that could possibly help us to sort out the Pardoner's more-than-Dostoevskian intermixture of supernatural faith and preternatural chicanery? Will semiotics or even Lacanian psycholinguistics anatomize Edmund for us, let alone Regan?

Either we become experiential critics when we read Chaucer and Shakespeare, or in too clear a sense we never read them at all. "Experiential" here necessarily means humane observation both of others and of ourselves, which leads to testing such observations in every context that indisputably is relevant. Longinus is the ancestor of such experiential criticism, but its masters are Samuel Johnson, Hazlitt and Emerson, Ruskin, Pater, and Wilde. A century gone mad on method has given us no critics to match these, nor are they likely to come again soon, though we still have Northrop Frye and Kenneth Burke, their last legitimate descendants.

IV

Mad on method, we have turned to rhetoric, and so much so that the best of us, the late Paul de Man, all but urged us to identify literature with rhetoric, so that criticism perhaps would become again the rhetoric of rhetoric, rather than a Burkean rhetoric of motives or a Fryean rhetoric of desires. Expounding the Nun's Priest's Tale, Talbot Donaldson points to "the enormous rhetorical elaboration of the telling" and is moved to a powerful insight into experiential criticism:

> Rhetoric here is regarded as the inadequate defense that mankind erects against an inscrutable reality; rhetoric enables man at best to regard himself as a being of heroic proportions—like Achilles, or like Chauntecleer—and at worst to maintain the last sad vestiges of his dignity (as a rooster Chauntecleer is carried in the fox's mouth, but as a hero he rides on his back), rhetoric enables man to find significance both in his desires and in his fate, and to pretend to himself that the universe takes him seriously. And rhetoric has a habit, too, of collapsing in the presence of simple common sense.

Yet rhetoric, as Donaldson implies, if it is Chaucer's rhetoric in particular, can be a life-enhancing as well as a life-protecting defense. Here is the heroic pathos of the Wife of Bath, enlarging existence even as she sums up its costs in one of those famous Chaucerian passages that herald Shakespearean exuberances to come:

> But Lord Crist, whan that it remembreth me
> Upon my youthe and on my jolitee,
> It tikleth me aboute myn herte roote—
> Unto this day it dooth myn herte boote
> That I have had my world as in my time.
> But age, allas, that al wol envenime,
> Hath me biraft my beautee and my pith—
> Lat go, farewel, the devel go therwith!
> The flour is goon, ther is namore to telle:
> The bren as I best can now moste I selle;
> But yit to be right merye wol I fonde.
>
> (*WBP,* l. 475; E. T. Donaldson, 2d ed.)

The defense against time, so celebrated as a defiance of time's revenges, is the Wife's fierce assertion also of the will to live at whatever expense. Rhetorically, the center of the passage is in the famously immense reverberation of her great cry of exultation and loss, "That I have had my world as in my time," where the double "my" is decisive, yet the "have had" falls away in a further intimation of mortality. Like Falstaff, the Wife is a grand trope of pathos, of life defending itself against every convention that would throw us into death-in-life. Donaldson wisely warns us that "pathos, however, must not be allowed to carry the day," and points to the coarse vigor of the Wife's final benediction to the tale she has told:

> And Jesu Crist us sende
> Housbondes meeke, yonge, and fresshe abedde—
> And grace t'overbide hem that we wedde.
> And eek I praye Jesu shorte hir lives
> That nought wol be governed by hir wives,
> And olde and angry nigardes of dispence—
> God sende hem soone a verray pestilence!
>
> (*WBT,* l. 402)

Blake feared the Wife of Bath because he saw in her what he called the Female Will incarnate. By the Female Will, Blake meant the will of the natural woman *or* the natural man, a prolepsis perhaps of Schopenhauer's rapacious Will to Live or Freud's "frontier concept" of the drive. Chaucer, I think, would not have quarreled with such an interpretation, but he would have scorned Blake's dread of the natural will or Schopenhauer's horror of its rapacity. Despite every attempt to assimilate him to a poetry of belief, Chaucer actually surpasses even Shakespeare as a celebrant of the natural heart, while like Shakespeare being beyond illusions concerning the merely natural. No great poet was less of a dualist than Chaucer was, and nothing makes poetry more difficult for critics, because all criticism is necessarily dualistic.

The consolation for critics and readers is that Chaucer and Shakespeare, Cervantes and Tolstoy, persuade us finally that everything remains to be done in the development of a criticism dynamic and comprehensive enough to represent such absolute writers without reduction or distortion. No codes or methods will advance the reading of Chaucer. The critic is thrown back upon herself or himself, and upon the necessity to become a vitalizing interpreter in the service of an art whose burden is only to carry more life forward into a time without boundaries.

Chaucer: Motive and Mask in the General Prologue

Ruth Nevo

The "National Portrait Gallery" theory of the General Prologue, so prevalent (if only as implicit assumption) in Chaucer criticism, is even on the face of it unlikely to be adequate. The claim, to take a fairly recent statement of it, is that Chaucer "presents his characters in the jumble and haphazardry of life . . . in a deliberately disordered chain" (Coghill). But this is art, not life; and an art as accomplished, subtle, and inclusive as Chaucer's is likely to be achieved as a result of deliberate order, not deliberate disorder. Chaucer's irony, moreover, as I shall try to show, is so often precisely not a function of local "tone of voice" that, unless it has the whole structure of the work to support it, it is apt in places to waver out of focus altogether; witness, for instance, such face-value readings of the Prioress as that of Kittredge.

Chaucer's method of characterization indeed has been a constant stumbling block to criticism. On the one hand, the astonishing individuality and variety—of behaviour, of posture, of complexion, even of finely discriminated and lovingly detailed articles of clothing—in the presentation of the pilgrims has tempted critics to regard them as sui generis, as gloriously capricious and unique "characters" in the English sense of "eccentrics." Kemp Malone takes this view, and explains it thus: "His pilgrims, if they were to be of interest to the reading public, had to be unusual, striking, remarkable in every possible way. . . . He makes no serious effort to be true to life, when he characterizes his pilgrims. One and all, they are too

From *The Modern Language Review* 58, no. 1 (January 1963).

good to be true. Such remarkable specimens of humanity as they are simply cannot be found in actual life." On the other hand, Chaucer's descriptive technique, which is based on the enumeration of objective detail and certainly establishes his vivid interest in the phenomenal world, has led other critics to claim "actual life" as his special sphere: so much so, indeed, as to make the documentation of the social history of England possible from his scrupulous record.

The sense of miscellany that the portrait-gallery theory registers is in fact contradicted at innumerable points by the presence of links of various kinds; and these, it is recognized, can only be operative within an overall composition. Critics are apt to ascribe their indubitable sense of such design in the whole work to the dramatic "plotting" of the intermitted narrative—the local motivation of each storyteller vis-à-vis his predecessor; or to the recurrent treatment of a common theme, as in the "marriage group" of stories and prologues; or to the pervasive presence of the sly spectator, Chaucer himself. But no one of these things, it is true, is sufficient to hold together in a unity of vision the mass of detail given in the Prologue.

Attempts have therefore been made to find such unity in the subject matter of *The Canterbury Tales* as a whole—the most elaborate arguing that the *Tales* were intended to treat in a systematic way the seven deadly sins, each Pilgrim representing the sin condemned in his tale. But this system breaks down over the whole series, and has been effectively refuted. If we are looking for a system which *The Canterbury Tales* will illustrate, we shall undoubtedly fail. But if the poem be allowed to project upon our minds its own internal system of contrasts, similarities, and recurrences, design will emerge. The poem will reveal itself not as a medley of spontaneous life, but as a masterpiece of stylized realism, controlled by a point of view from which the world could be interrupted and represented in its double aspect as random actuality and ordered meaning.

It is as well to remember afresh that "the latter half of the fourteenth century was more consciously artistic, more secure in command of its resources, than any other period till the time of Pope." (W. P. Ker, *Essays on Medieval Literature*). This means that Chaucer was writing for a highly cultivated audience, an audience sufficiently sophisticated to demand and appreciate the obliqueness of consummate literary art. The Prologue is a vivid representation of everyday life from a vantage point "above" the level of the life described, and so commanding the perspective, the suggestion of multiple possibilities, which the careful craft of nuance and ironic insinuation can give. Chaucer's characterization is thus not directly transcribed from life, artlessly vivid, but mediate, elaborately constructed and containing within itself, in the careful placing and allocation of elements, implicit moral evaluation. The moral insight, moreover, gives rise, in the Prologue to *The Canterbury Tales,* to an analysis of social rank in terms of economic behaviour which is remarkable for its penetration and its prescience.

II

As we read the Prologue we become aware of a certain family resemblance between the pilgrims, despite their diversity. Or rather, as character is subtly, almost imperceptibly revealed, we become aware of a persistent criterion of selection operating upon the data provided by observation. It is not, of course, that every objective detail given in the description is chosen according to this single principle. What we do find is that there is no portrait, however short, without its reference, direct or indirect, to the matter of money. The pilgrim's characteristic behaviour is defined in every case in terms of the acquisition and use of wealth. The "goodness" of the good characters, and the "badness" of the bad or questionable characters are both exhibited with reference to this criterion, and in the characters towards whom there is an ironic attitude the irony inheres in the evident discrepancy between profession and action with regard to this same matter. Since there is little, save sex, in social life more productive of diverse possibility on the one hand, nor on the other more readily susceptible to overriding moral judgement, than the individual's attitude to his worldly goods, or his status in terms of worldly goods, such an analysis has the double advantage of a fixed point and a spectrum. Money—pelf—is the touchstone to which each of these characters is brought, and by which he is tested. There is no portrait which does not take its orientation from an attitude to money or from dealings with money, whether in the form of illicit gain or of legitimate hire.

It is not only the Doctor, who loved gold in special because gold in physic is a cordial; in the house of the hospitable Franklin it snows meat and drink; and the Merchant's success, it is slyly and acutely implied, is due to his skill in not letting anyone know when he is in debt, while his interest in the "keeping of the Sea" between Middleburgh and Orewelle is patently not purely patriotic. Furthermore, whether he is a Merchant Adventurer, or a Stapler exporting wool, illicit currency deals are apparently a mainstay of his business. The Shipman can be trusted in charge of craft in difficult seas and has moreover sufficiently his wits about him to draw a draught of wine while the Chapman sleeps; the "sclendre cholerich" Reeve knows well enough how to feather his own nest, while attending to his master's affairs, as his own "faire wonying" shows; and his colleague, the Manciple, knows better than any of the students of the Middle Temple how to make a spendthrift nobleman's budget balance. The Friar's *In Principio* is so effective that it is able to extract the last farthing from a poor widow; the Prioress's penchant for high life extends to the choice and costly fare—roasted flesh, milk and wastel bread—on which her "smale houndes" are fed; the Monk quite blatantly spares no expense either upon his table or his stable. The wives of the Guildsmen, those fair burgesses, are not averse to being called Madame and leading the procession to vigils, privileges they enjoy by virtue of their husbands' "catel and rente"; and these respectable aldermen, together with the Cook, worthy, to judge from the delicacies he provides, of his temporary hire, are contrasted with the rumbustious Miller, the stout Carl who is master of the art of stealing corn and taking triple toll for grinding. The Lawyer, besides being well provided with fees, and robes, by his clients, is a great purchaser of land, of which he invariably succeeds in getting unrestricted possession. That precious pair, the Summoner and the Pardoner, will be treated separately; here it is perhaps enough to point out the Summoner's way with the archdeacon's curse (ll. 653ff.), and the quite unironical flat statement in the Pardoner's portrait,

> But with thise relikes, whan that he had fond
> A povre person dwellynge up-on lond,
> Up-on a day he gat him moore moneye
> Than that the person gat in monthes tweye.
> And thus, with feyned flaterye and japes,
> He made the person and the peple his apes.
>
> (l. 701; F. N. Robinson, 2d ed.)

The Parson, to turn to the credit side of the human balance-sheet, is "a good shepherd and no mercenarie"; the Plowman a good worker, living in peace and charity, working often without hire to help others, paying his own tithes faithfully; the Student's single coat is threadbare because he is too unworldly to get him a benefice; the Knight's coat, on the other hand, is still stained by the armour of his service in the cause of God. His son, to be sure, is a fashionable young man, but his courtesy is of the kind which by long-accepted definition is untouched by shadow of lucre, as is the yeoman service of the sturdy green-clad forester who is his retainer.

All these people have, of course, other and various attributes: they are sly, lecherous, quarrelsome, bawdy, vain, cheerful; and the stars in their courses have had much to do with their dispositions and predispositions.

But their *motivation* springs from a single source—Mammon; and it is this which provides the dynamic of the Prologue to *The Canterbury Tales* and the master key to its design.

III

Chaucer had been a page at court in his youth and an ambassador in his maturity. He had spent twelve years as Controller of Customs, had contracted economic enterprises as Clerk of Works, and had managed a great estate in his capacity as deputy forester of the royal forest of North Petherton. These were excellent vantage points from which to take in the economic structure of his society and the economic nature of its trades and professions. The degree to which what one may call the canny bourgeois attitude to the importance of money in determining life is marked in the Prologue can be gauged from a comparison with the tale of *Sir Gawayn and the Green Knight,* a roughly contemporary work which matches Chaucer's in the fineness and complexity of its organization. In the world of Gawayn wealth exists indeed, but only to be spent in honourable and conspicuous consumption. On the one occasion when a gift is refused, because of its value, the significance of the whole exchange is in a point of honour.

But Chaucer's achievement is far more than the satirical reflexions of a canny bourgeois, or an observant man of affairs. Money is the leitmotif of his design; but to find the whole shape and scope of his conception, it is necessary to turn to his dramatis personae, his "cast in the order of appearance," and to ask, as one would ask of any contemporary work of fiction, what the author wishes to imply by this particular choice and arrangement of the human scene. We will find, I believe, a fusion of two things: an acutely original analysis of a society in which commerce is just emerging from feudalism, and the disciplined vision of a tolerant but uncompromising moral sensibility.

The cast in order of appearance is as follows: Knight; Squire; Yeoman; Prioress; Monk; Nun's Priest; Merchant; Clerk; Lawyer; Franklin; The Cloth Guildsmen; Cook; Ship's Captain; Doctor; Wife of Bath; Parson; Plowman; Miller; Manciple; Reeve; Summoner; Pardoner. The suggestion of a scale of social rank shading through from the upper classes of society to the lower is irresistible, but it encounters several obstacles to complete consistency. Why, for instance, is the mendicant Friar way up above the wealthy Merchant? This suggests a religious–secular grouping, which, however, is not carried through. Or why again is that unsavoury ecclesiastic, the Pardoner, below the Plowman? Is there a moral criterion at work here? But the creator of the good Parson, who comes between the merry Monk and the pernicious Pardoner, could hardly be, and is not, simply equating rank with virtue. It is at this point, no doubt, that one is tempted by the "deliberate jumble" view, especially when one remembers that in *The Parlement of Foules* Chaucer had no difficulty in presenting, with the greatest liveliness and conviction, the social hierarchy of his day. Here, indeed, is the heart of the matter. In the *Parlement* is reflected the conventional feudal stratification of society into gentle and simple on the basis of birth, nurture and prestige. In the Prologue to the *Tales* there is a new hypothesis: a classification of society based upon the various sources of income.

The Knight heads the list as the warrior member of the landowning feudal aristocracy. With him appear his son, the Squire, and the Yeoman; the latter is not characterized except as a member of the Knight's retinue, but as such sufficiently underlines the aristocratic nature of the ménage. They are followed by the Prioress, the Monk and the Friar. If we remember the vast wealth with which Henry VIII rewarded his courtiers when he dissolved the monasteries, we shall not be surprised to find these three next on a scale of wealth and power—not indeed as personal possessors of wealth, but as members of the great propertied religious houses and orders. The Merchant, the Student, the Lawyer, and the Franklin fall naturally into the next group: the well-to-do or—in the case of the Student, who is in fact without office and poor—the potentially well-to-do. To this day the City man, the gentleman owner of an estate in the country, and the barrister belong to the upper middle class in England; and the validity of this grouping is confirmed by the placing next of the Guildsmen, the Cook, the Ship's Captain, the Doctor and the Tradesman's wife—the lower middle class. Since medieval times, the doctor has gone up in the social scale and joined the middle or even upper middle free professions, but the city artisans and tradesmen, the master mariner, the master chef, will still use the tradesmen's entrance, and the standing of the medieval leech or barber-surgeon is exactly reflected here. The Parson, that humblest rung of the ecclesiastical ladder, is of peasant origin—as he is so often, even in modern times, in Italy and Central Europe. His brother the Plowman stands at the solid base of the whole order of society. He is the agricultural labourer, probably a small tenant farmer, of villein ancestry but of sufficient independence now. Nicely juxtaposed between the peasant and the final group stands the Miller—like the former and the latter, of villein origin, but, through his cherished right to run a mill, freed from the bonds of feudal dependence. The last group, the Manciple, Reeve, Summoner, and Pardoner, are the most interestingly placed and argue most cogently for Chaucer's economic insight.

Coghill distinguishes between what he calls the upper servants, the Manciple and the Reeve, and the lower servants, the Yeoman and the Cook, while the Pardoner and the Summoner coming "at an infinite moral and social depth below all these . . . (were) laymen, hangers-on of the Church, and hated." However, Chaucer's treatment of the Knight's servant, the Yeoman, is so qualitatively different from his treatment of these four that one cannot escape the sense of a profound distinction. They are among his most fully drawn characters and the targets of his sharpest irony. In the Summoner's portrait is found one of Chaucer's most barbed shafts:

> And if he foond o-wher a good felawe,
> He wolde techen him to have noon awe,
> In swich caas, of the ercedeknes curs,
> But-if a mannes soule were in his purs;
> For in his purs he sholde y-punisshed be.
> 'Purs is the ercedeknes helle,' seyde he.
>
> (l. 653)

Chaucer adds, in mock unawareness of the Summoner's pocket-lining motive in this transaction, and as if concerned only with purity of doctrine in respect of archidiaconal powers:

> But wel I woot he lyed right in dede;
> Of cursyng oghte ech gilty man him drede,
> For curs wol slee right as assoillyng savith,
> And also war hym of a *Significavit*.
>
> (l. 661)

With regard to the Reeve, he takes care to imply that his craft-carpentry, which he had learned in his youth, proved less profitable than his later art of subtly pleasing his master, while of the profits accumulated by the Pardoner from his "craft" we are left in no doubt whatever. All caterers, we are told, could well take a leaf from the book of the Manciple:

> For wheither that he payde or took by taille,
> Algate he wayted so in his achaat,
> That he was ay biforn and in good staat.
>
> (l. 570)

Chaucer's tongue is so unobtrusively in his cheek that the statement can almost be taken in perfect innocence. But "wayten" has (according to

Robinson) the meanings "to show," or "to put upon," as well as "to observe" or "to watch."

These four are of peasant origin. The Reeve was originally elected by the hinds from their number to deal with the lord of the estate. They have in fact gravitated from the ranks of the labourers to those of salaried officials, or upper servants, of an estate or an institution; their income is derived neither from property, nor commerce, nor argricultural labour, but from "negotiation," for wages, and inevitably therefore, from graft. All abuse their office in a way that the craftsman servant (the Cook) or the personal servant (the Yeoman) are not able to do. The "infinite moral and social depth" mentioned by Coghill is not the result of their being laymen, hangers-on of the Church, and hated—this would in any case not apply to the Reeve and Manciple; it is a direct function of their peculiarly parasitic position in society.

What we have, then, is a clear, socioeconomic ranking based upon an analysis of the origins of income, with the characters who are presented as moral standards, or ideal types, namely, Knight, Plowman, Parson, each placed on the humblest, the most productive and serviceable rung of their respective functional orders—the warriors, the workers, and the worshippers.

On this view of Chaucer's idea, moreover, the placing of the two youths in the party presents them in a significantly ambiguous light. Their youth makes their final destination an open question, as it were. The Clerk's function as student makes him a potential wielder of power and influence, whether in the secular or religious sphere; he is youthfully resolved—for the present at any rate—to pursue the things of the spirit at the expense of those of the world. The Squire, the younger generation of knighthood, decked in his fashionable finery, elegantly accomplished and gaily amorous, is nevertheless lowly and serviceable to his father, and may well become, like him, a sturdy and devoted defender of the faith. But it is equally possible, with no great flight of the historical imagination, to see in this young man the ancestor of the Elizabethan or Restoration fop, or the spendthrift young heir who was the later prey of the London sharks.

IV

It has often been remarked that Chaucer chose, as with a stroke of genius, the only two places in England where this multifarious throng would all be likely to meet on equal terms—an Inn and a Cathedral; and the circumstance—a pilgrimage—which could credibly unite them in a common purpose.

Yet the idea of the pilgrimage is even more important to the conception and design of *The Canterbury Tales* than such a comment gives reason to think. On the supposition that Chaucer wished merely to paint a national portrait gallery and accordingly "chose to measure the world by its smiling self rather than by the Kingdom of Heaven" (Coghill), the pilgrimage has indeed no more than an accidental value in providing a common meeting place and a common journey. It can be argued, however, that it is, on the contrary, quintessential, being the structural frame within which the Chaucerian irony operates, and a chief means whereby Chaucer reveals that it was in fact by the Kingdom of Heaven that he was measuring his world.

For that which, as we have seen, serves as a constant principle of selection in the descriptive portraits, serves also as a constant criterion of moral judgement operative throughout the General Prologue. Every character passes, or does not pass, the test of worldliness. The cavalcade unrolls before our eyes, detail after detail falls subtly, unerringly into place and we become aware of a universal category. They are worldlings, worldlings all. Save for the defender of the faith, the good pastor, the honest plowman, and the patient, unworldly scholar, these Canterbury pilgrims in festive journey to a Christian martyr's shrine, are totally taken up with the world and the flesh. They are worldlings in the fullest sense of the word—adjusted to the world, committed to the world, worldly wise. The world is their natural element. But it is within the framework of the pilgrimage that the dimension of irony is added to the meticulous descriptions. Not a word is lost, not an item wasted in the presence of the uncompromising fact represented by Canterbury.

The irony, so elusive as to have eluded many an honest critic, has been found special enough to merit the defining adjective "Chaucerian." Its mechanism is deceptively simple, its force the result of absolute consistency. Locally, in each portrait, it is the views and standards and criteria of the world that are assumed. The Prioress's fine manners, the Monk's fat swans and "deynte" horses, the Merchant's "chevysaunce," the Wife of Bath's magnificent kerchiefs, the Summoner's good fellowship—these in the eyes of the world are no great matter, are even desirable values. But at certain significant points—the Wife of Bath so wroth that she was out of all charity if preceded in the procession to offering; or *Amor vincit omnia*; or the Kingdom of Mammon again and again in an unremitting iteration; or the presence of the virtuous, the pure in spirit, the unmercenary—these views, standards and criteria are set by implication in absolute opposition to another absolute demand:

> The hye God, on whom that we bileeve
> In wilful poverte chees to lyve his lyf.

Chaucer is tolerant of his worldlings, profoundly so, but with a tolerance which is not moral leniency. It does not spring from a desire to excuse or mitigate their worldliness: there is no question, for instance, of his exonerating the Monk's travesty of the cloister in the name of gracious living. Such venial "tolerance" is no part of Chaucer's moral sensibility. Nor is it indeed part of the moral sensibility of an age which witnessed the Lollard risings, and more than once records its own version of puritan strictness of conscience. His tolerance has deeper roots—in a profound and equable conviction of human frailty. Irony, not invective, is his medium; and it implies no compromise. And the famous geniality springs not from whatever may be understood by such much used phrases as "warm humanity" or "love of life" but from the serenity of a perfect sense of moral proportion, and from joy in the exercise of a crystal-clear intelligence and a mastered literary art.

The intensity of the irony in the portraits is a function of the degree of discrepancy between profession and action in each of the characters portrayed. Chaucer evidently expects less from a Miller or a Man of Law than from a Prioress, a Monk or a Pardoner. Nevertheless the two possibilities, of virtue and of corruption, are constantly entertained of cleric and layman alike; and it is in this connexion that the continuity of the Mammon theme performs its remarkable double service. It links the universe of socioeconomic actualities to the universe of moral values. For while corruption shows itself in the abuse or exploitation of a socioeconomic function this is the local and particular expression of a more general evil, which is operative in the structure of private personality before it manifests itself in the performance of public office. It was defined by Shelley as "the principle of self of which money is the visible incarnation." Cupidity is its best name, a conception more inclusive than greed or avarice, and one which can easily and justly be conveyed by the images of getting and spending, images through which it is focused though not exhausted.

The Wife of Bath may stand as the garrulous spokesman for all the weaker brethren among her fellow travellers. She has her own rights in the long debate on the virtue of women which links several of the tales. But no one would claim that her version of married bliss exemplifies the principle of self transcended. When, on the other hand, she argues that virginity is great perfection—for those who wish to be perfect—she exemplifies the easygoing conscience of the majority of the pilgrims. Once the self permits its own exclusion from the moral order it itself acknowledges, the essential breach is made, and the way is open for every kind of cupidity and every kind of rationalization. The way of this world is a practical application of Lear's thundered forbearance, "None does offend, none I say, none." But Lear was mad. His mind had broken down under the stress of unaccustomed insight. These pious pilgrims are as sane as can be, and no doctrine could better suit their lax, self-palliating souls. They have all excluded themselves from the rules. Self-indulgent cupidity is the law of their being, and the pursuit of pelf, with all that goes along with it, its chief and most prominent manifestation in the context of social relations. On this view, of course, Chaucer's apology for his neglect of rank is ironic. Whatever the prejudices and preconceptions of readers, *he* will exclude no one from the indictment on account of his rank.

Thus is the pilgrimage revealed as a masquerade. We think we are being offered "characters" in their habit as they lived. And so we are, down to the very warts on their noses. But the warts in Chaucer are not mere random "realism." They are part of a deliberate strategy whereby we do not notice, until it is borne in on us with powerful obliqueness, that we are witnessing, not a depiction of personality, but an unmasking of self—the very inner self. We have our clues in the Prologue to warn us of the fact that all is not quite as it seems. In the *Tales*—in those of them at any rate which do seem to be linked to their tellers and their prologues—we have the naked truth. The relationship between tale and teller is not the kind of psychological projection which a modern conception of characterization would demand. The technique is in one sense, more primitive than that, akin to the aside or the informative soliloquy of the Elizabethan drama, in which the character unmasks himself (neither wittingly nor unwittingly—his degree of consciousness is irrelevant) in direct revelation to the audience.

It is doubly ironic that the master of ceremonies, the critic-unmasker, the poet Chaucer, appears himself masked in the masquerade. Or rather, it is a necessary functional device that he should do so, for his mask of the innocent, the simpleton, is the means whereby he can present in seemingly unsuspecting acceptance, the worldly scale of values of the pilgrims. He takes them at their face value, the value they put upon themselves. He is all seriousness. He thinks it a great pity that the Cook has a running sore on his leg; he thinks there is much to be said for the Monk's arguments against Austin; he is sure the Summoner makes a great mistake in underestimating the effectiveness of archdeacons' "curses"; he finds the Prioress a very pretty lady, and ever so well bred. Only in the case of the Pardoner does he cross the strict bounds of politeness. And little wonder. For the Pardoner stands at the outer pale of Chaucer's tolerance for humanity. He is a concentrate of the maximum rapacity and the maximum hypocrisy. He is parasite of parasites. His tale is the most haunting and powerful of "moralities"; and its text is *Radix malorum est cupiditas.*

Medieval Estates Satire and the General Prologue

Jill Mann

It is a cliché of Chaucer criticism that the Canterbury pilgrims are both individuals and types. But this critical unanimity coexists with striking divergencies on what constitutes the typical or the individual.

One could begin by suggesting that the "individual" quality is that which distinguishes one person from other people. But this cannot be a single character trait, since financial greed, for example, is a feature of both Friar and Pardoner. Is individuality constituted by the peculiar *combination* of traits? Unfortunately, this is precisely what some critics take to be the typical. For example, Root thought that the combination of "individualising traits" in the Prioress's portrait suggests "that type which finds fullest realisation in the head of a young lady's school." The "individual" is then reduced to the level of "a local habitation and a name"; "the Wife of Bath is typical of certain primary instincts of woman, but she is given local habitation 'bisyde Bath,' and is still further individualised by her partial deafness and the peculiar setting of her teeth."

J. L. Lowes also seemed to accept that "the typical" refers to general outlines of personality when he praises "the delicate balance between the *character*, in the technical, Theophrastian sense of the word, and the *individual*—a balance which preserves at once the typical qualities of the one and the human idiosyncrasies of the other." However, Lowes' "human idiosyncrasies" suggest something different from the isolated physical traits to which Root attributes the individualisation of the pilgrims; and indeed

---

From *Chaucer and Medieval Estates Satire: The Literature of Social Classes and the General Prologue to the* Canterbury Tales.

concrete details, such as the Yeoman's clothing, can help to realise an estates type.

Agreement on the nature of the typical is no greater than on that of the individual. Speirs, for example, classifies the characters at times by social situation (the Squire is "the eternal young bachelor," the Yeoman "simply a solid English countryman," the Clerk is "the unworldly scholar of all time," the Pardoner is "the eternal cheapjack at the fair whose impudence and success never fail to fascinate and amaze"), and at times by moral qualities ("Gluttony underlies the Frankeleyn, Avarice the Doctor of Physic"). Baldwin attempts a sort of ad hoc isolation of what he calls the "radix traits" of the characters:

> the Knight can be described by "worthynesse," the Squire by "youth," the Yeoman by "forester," and the Prioress by "noblesse oblige." The Wife of Bath may be summed up by "archwife" of disposition, eye and conversation; the Monk by "game" . . . ; the Friar by "wantonnesse," the Merchant by "façade," and the Parson by "pastoral activity."

Faced with this plethora of conceptions of "type," I have preferred [in *Chaucer and Medieval Estates Satire*] not to attempt another way of defining or describing the typical and the individual, but to work on lines similar to those suggested by R. M. Lumiansky's terms: "the expected and the unexpected." Rather than trying to decide whether a character corresponds to a credible combination of personality traits, rooted in the eternal aspects of human nature, I have tried to consider how far the information given about him accords with the expectations raised by his introduction as "a knight" or "a monk." The results of this consideration have shown that the estates type was the basis for Chaucer's creation of the Canterbury pilgrims. But the accompanying analysis of the style in which Chaucer presents the estates type has also shown that the answer to the question "are the pilgrims individuals or types?" would vary according to whether it was based on source material or the reader's impression.

In the past, there seems to have been an assumption that the effect of the Prologue's material would be identical with the source from which it was drawn: if the portraits were drawn observations of real individuals, they would suggest these individuals to Chaucer's audience; if they were drawn from social satire, they would convey the impression of moralised types. The same assumption encouraged critics to see the union of type and individual in terms of the combination of well-known features of certain social classes with invented details. Thus Lumiansky goes on to say of the

Knight: "As a result of a combination of expected and unexpected traits, he assumes memorable individuality in the mind of the reader." But our chapter on the Knight has shown that the qualities Lumiansky finds unexpected in "a professional military man"—the fact that he is "prudent, humble, circumspect in speech, modest in dress, and serious in religious devotion"—would not be at all unexpected in the stereotyped ideal of his estate. The preceding chapters have also shown that it is not the *concreteness* of invented or unexpected details (where we do find them) which produces individuality, for they are not essentially different from the concrete details that are a traditional part of estates satire. Moreover, invented details are used to extend the typical, just as well as the individual, aspects of a character.

A hint of the means by which Chaucer persuades us that the pilgrims *are* individuals—that they exist as independent people—is however given in Lumiansky's comment that the terminology of "the expected and the unexpected" "has the advantage of placing the emphasis upon the reader's reaction to the technique." This emphasis I believe to be correct, and I have tried to show that our strong impression of the individuality of the figures in the Prologue is due to the fact that Chaucer encourages us to *respond* to them as individuals. Their "individuality" lies in the techniques whereby Chaucer elicits from us a reaction, whether complicated or unequivocal, similar to the reactions aroused in us by real-life individuals.

We have already seen [elsewhere] what these techniques are. Chaucer calls forth contradictory responses—a positive emotional or sensuous response, conflicting with an expectation that moral disapproval is called for—in order to make us feel the complexity of his characters. He makes us uncertain of the "facts" that lie behind their social or professional façades. He uses a sense of past experience, discernible from present appearance, personality or behaviour, to give us the conviction that his characters are not eternal abstractions but are affected by time. And he incorporates an awareness of their point of view—their reactions to the traditional attitudes to their existence, their terminology and standards of judgement—which also gives us a strong sense of their independent life. Chaucer forces us to feel that we are dealing with real people because we cannot apply to them the absolute reponses appropriate to the abstractions of moralistic satire.

We may also make some suggestions about the different functions of the "typical" and "individual" aspects of the characters. This is left rather vague by some critics; Root, for example, remarked that the combination of individual and typical in the portraits makes them more effective, but did not say why, nor what they are effectively doing. One reason why

Chaucer is at pains to give his characters "life" as individuals is obviously that they are to act as individuals in the drama of the *Canterbury Tales;* they talk and react to each other as individual human beings would do. The "individual" aspect is therefore vital to the frame of the tales. The "typical" aspect is, however, equally vital to Chaucer's purpose in the whole work. The most obvious aspect of the *Canterbury Tales,* even in its incomplete state, is its comprehensiveness. It clearly aims at universality, at taking up all the themes and styles of contemporary literature and making one glorious compendium of them. The Prologue in a sense constitutes a kind of sample of what is to follow by its wide range of tone and mood. The serious ideals—chivalric, religious, labouring—which operate in the portraits of Knight, Parson and Ploughman, furnish a serious tone in addition to the comic and savage ones on which Chaucer can draw in the main body of his work. But as well as this, the Prologue makes its own contribution to the genres included in the *Canterbury Tales,* by the clear reference to estates literature in its form and content. It is especially appropriate that estates literature should perform this introductory function, since it lays claim to a universality of its own, and since its subject matter is the whole society, the "raw material" from which the other genres select their own areas of interest.

The *Canterbury Tales,* however, is not a compendium of literary genres in any simple sense. The method of the work is not additive, but dialectic; the tales modify and even contradict each other, exploring subjects in a way that emphasises their different and opposed implications. Sometimes we can follow the development of one theme through various mutations; even where the unifying theme is absent, it is noteworthy that the stimulus for tale-telling is the quarrel. The overall effect of this process of exploring tensions and contradictions is to relativise our values until we reach the absolute values of the Parson, who is willing to admit of no compromise or modification—but in assigning these absolute values to a character *within* the *Tales* (and, moreover, not to the narrator) Chaucer in one sense makes these values relative too.

The same refusal to take up an absolute standpoint can be found in the Prologue. One important demonstration of this has emerged [in *Chaucer and Medieval Estates Satire*] from a comparison with other estates material—the fact that the persons who suffer from behaviour attributed to some of the pilgrims are left out of account—what I have called "omission of the victim." I have already stressed the importance of not letting our awareness of these victims, an awareness for which other satiric works are responsible, lead us into supplying them in the Prologue for the purposes of making a moral judgement, whether on Prioress, Merchant, Lawyer or Doctor. Chaucer deliberately omits them in order to encourage us to see the behaviour of the pilgrims from their own viewpoints, and to ignore what they necessarily ignore in following their courses of action. Of course, our blindness differs from theirs in being to some extent voluntary—for the pilgrims' viewpoint is not maintained everywhere in the Prologue—while their blindness is unconscious and a condition of their existence. The manipulation of viewpoint, and ignorance (wilful or unconscious), are traditionally taken as features of irony, and the omission of the victim is a functional part of the ironic tone of the Prologue. The tone, as we have noted, becomes more forthright and moves away from irony precisely at moments when we are made conscious of the victim, and in particular of the victim's attitude to the pilgrim.

The omission of the victim is part of the Prologue's peculiar social ethic, which extends even to the pilgrims that Chaucer presents as morally admirable. The Yeoman, for example, is certainly an honest and hardworking member of his profession. Yet fault has been found even with him, on the grounds that

> no practical application of his skill is indicated. . . . The description stops short at the means, the end is never indicated. The result is the impression of a peculiarly truncated consciousness.
>
> (M. F. Bovill, unpublished thesis)

As regards the particular portrait, this interpretation is surely mistaken; there is no criticism of the Yeoman as an individual. The comment may, however, usefully focus attention on the small part played by social ends in the Prologue. This has already been indicated in discussion of the individual portraits. The *effects* of the Knight's campaigning, of the Merchant's "chevisaunce," of the Sergeant's legal activities, even of the Doctor's medicine, are not what Chaucer has in mind when he assures us of their professional excellence. It is by ignoring effects that he can present the expertise of his rogues on the same level as the superlative qualities of his admirable figures. His ultimate purpose in this is not to convey any naive enthusiasm for people, nor comic effect, although the Prologue is of course rich in comedy, nor is it even a "connoisseur's appreciation of types," although this attitude characterises the narrator's ironic pose in presenting the individual estates. The overall effect of this method is rather to sharpen our perceptions of the basis of everyday attitudes to people, of the things we take into account and of the things we willingly ignore.

We may clarify this by pointing out that the distinction between Langland and Chaucer is not just, as is usually assumed, the distinction between a religious and a secular writer, between didacticism and comedy. It is true that Langland and most of the army of estates writers before him, have a continual sense of the rewards of Heaven and the punishments of Hell, which of itself provides a "reason" for moral behaviour, and that this sense is lacking in Chaucer. But it is also true that Langland shows, in passages such as the ploughing of Piers's half-acre, the practical bases for, and effects of, specific moral injunctions, while Chaucer has no *systematic* platform for moral values, not even an implicit one, in the Prologue.

When we first compare Langland and Chaucer, there is a temptation to conclude as Manly did, that Chaucer's satire is convincing because

> he does not argue, and there is no temptation to refute him. He does not declaim, and there is no opportunity for reply. He merely lets us see his fools and rascals in their native foolishness and rascality, and we necessarily think of them as he would have us think.
>
> *(New Light)*

Undoubtedly it is true that Chaucer not only persuades us that fools and rascals can be very charming people, but is at the same time taking care to make us suspect that they are fools and rascals. If, however, we examine more closely what considerations determine what "he would have us think" of the pilgrims, we find that they are not always moral ones. For example, if we compare the portraits of the Friar and the Summoner, we find that many of the faults we attribute to them are identical: fondness of drink; parade of pretended knowledge; sexual licence and the corruption of young people; the encouragement of sinners to regard money-payments as adequate for release from sin. Yet what is our attitude to them? I think it is true to say that our judgement on the Friar is less harsh than our disgust for the Summoner. The reasons for this, in a worldly sense, are perfectly adequate; the Friar's "pleasantness" is continually stressed, he makes life easy for everyone, is a charming companion, has musical talent, he has a white neck and twinkling eyes and good clothes, while the Summoner revolts the senses with his red spotted face and the reek of garlic and onions. But although adequate to account for our reactions, these considerations are not in any sense moral ones.

It is sometimes said that the physical appearance of the Summoner symbolises his inner corruption; there is certainly a link between physical ugliness and spiritual ugliness in other, moralising writers. But Chaucer is, as it were, turning their procedure round in order to point to its origins in our irrational, instinctive reactions. The explicit moralising attitude to beauty and ugliness—that they are irrelevant beside considerations of moral worth—coexists, paradoxically, with an implicit admission of their relevance in the use of aesthetic imagery to recommend moral values. In the *Ancrene Wisse,* for example, the author associates beautiful scents, jewels and so on, with heavenly values, and stinks and ugliness with the devil; he then finds himself in the difficult position of trying to encourage an ascetic indifference to *real* bad smells. Chaucer makes this tension between moral judgement and instinctive emotional reaction into a central feature of the Prologue partly in order to create the ambiguity and complexity of response which persuades us that the characters are complex individuals, but at the same time to show us, in the Prologue, what *are* the grounds for our like or dislike of our neighbours. Moral factors have a part in our judgement, but on a level with other, less "respectable" considerations. There is no hesitation in admiring the unquestioned moral worth of the Knight or Parson, but this will not prevent us from enjoying the company of rogues with charm, or despising those who have no mitigating graces.

I shall return in a moment to the significance of this lack of systematically expressed values, after noting some other means which produce it. The first of these again emerges in contrast to estates material, and consists of the simple but vivid similes which run through some of the portraits—head shining like glass, eyes twinkling like stars—and which plays a large part in convincing us of the attractiveness of such figures as the Monk and the Friar. The constant use of this sort of comparison creates a tone which is at once relaxed, colloquial and animated—the kind of style which, as Derek Brewer has pointed out, finds its best counterpart in the English romances, and which differs strikingly from the taut, pointed style of learned satire. Another type of simile is neutral or explanatory—"As brood as is a bokeler or a targe"—and occasional examples of this sort may be found in French or Anglo-Norman satire. But the first group, in which the stress on attractiveness runs counter to the critical effect of the satire, would destroy the intention of a moralising satirist. A writer like Langland deals in occasional vivid imagery, but its effect usually works together with the moral comment.

> And *as a leke hadde yleye* · *longe in the sonne*
> So loked he with lene chekes · lourynge foule.
>
> And *as a letheren purs* · lolled his chekes.

Occasionally the imagery works *with* the moral comment in the General Prologue also; we have noted that the animal imagery in the portraits of the Miller, Pardoner and Summoner persuades us that we are dealing with crude or unpleasant personalities. In both kinds of usage, the imagery does not reflect moral comment so much as create it; and the contradictory ways in which it is used means that it is also working to destroy the *systematic* application of moral judgements.

The role of the narrator and the use of irony in the Prologue have received abundant comments, but they can in this connection take on a new light. It is the narrator who himself constantly identifies with the pilgrim's point of view—and that means the point of view of his estate—and encourages us to see the world from this angle. Even when the narrator distinguishes the pilgrim's view from his own, this also, paradoxically, makes us sharply aware of the series of insights into estates consciousness that we are given, and of the tension between their perspectives and our own which is implied in the "his" of such phrases as "his bargaynes."

Moreover, the narrator acts as a representative for the rest of society in its relation to each estate. In this role, he shows us how often the rest of society is not allowed to go beyond the professional façade, to know what is the truth, or to apply any absolute values to professional behaviour. We are in a world of "experts," where the moral views of the layman become irrelevant. The narrator assumes that each pilgrim is an expert, and presents him in his own terms, according to his own values, in his own language. All excellence becomes "tricks of the trade"—and this applies to the Parson's virtues as well as to the Miller's thefts. In the Prologue we are in a world of means rather than ends. A large part of the narrator's criteria for judging people then becomes their success in social relationships at a *personal* level; they are judged on pleasantness of appearance, charm of manner, social accomplishments. Their social role is reduced to a question of sociability.

These criteria are of course ironically adopted, and we must therefore ask what is the significance of Chaucer's use of irony in the Prologue. We can take as starting point the definition of irony offered by the thirteenth-century rhetorician Buoncompagno de Signa:

> Yronia enim est plana et demulcens verborum positio cum indignatione animi et subsannatione . . . Ceterum vix aliquis adeo fatuus reperitur qui non intelligat si de eo quod non est conlaudetur. Nam si commendares Ethyopem de albedine, latronem de custodia, luxuriosum de castitate, de facili gressu claudum, cecum de visu, pauperem de divitiis, et servum de libertate, stuperent inenarrabili dolore laudati, immo vituperati, quia nil aliud est vituperium quam alicuius malefacta per contrarium commendare vel iocose narrare.

> (Irony is the bland and sweet use of words to convey disdain and ridicule . . . Hardly anyone can be found who is so foolish that he does not understand if he is praised for what he is not. For if you should praise the Ethiopian of his whiteness, the thief for his guardianship, the lecher for his chastity, the lame for his agility, the blind for his sight, the pauper for his riches, and the slave for his liberty, they would be struck dumb with inexpressible grief to have been praised, but really vituperated, for it is nothing but vituperation to commend the evil deeds of someone through their opposite, or to relate them wittily.)
>
> (trans. after J. F. Benton)

This definition is a useful starting point, precisely because it does *not* fit Chaucer's habitual use of irony. For what he does so often is to commend the lecher, not for chastity, but for lechery—to enthuse, in fact, over his being the most lecherous lecher of all.

It is true that at certain moments Chaucer seems to be praising someone "per contrarium"; we think of the "gentil Pardoner." But in making his definition, Buoncompagno assumes that the truth about the person ironically described is always clear to us; we know that an Ethiopian is really black. The baffling feature of the Prologue, as we have seen, is how often it weakens our grasp of the truth about a character, even while suggesting that it is somehow at odds with the narrator's enthusiastic praise. We begin to wonder whether the Ethiopian was not after all born of colonial parents, and white. . . .

The same characteristics of Chaucerian irony are revealed if we analyse it in terms of a modern definition. Earle Birney suggests that the concept of irony always implies the creation of the illusion that a real incongruity or conflict does not exist, and that this illusion is so shaped that the bystander may, immediately or ultimately, see through it, and be thereby surprised into a more vivid awareness of the very conflict. A large part in the creation and dispersal of the illusion in this ironic process in the Prologue is played by the narrator and the shifting attitudes he adopts. The shift can be sharp:

> Nowher so bisy a man as he ther nas,
> And yet he semed bisier than he was
>
> (ll. 320–21; F. N. Robinson, 2d ed.)

or it can be more subtle, as in the case with Chaucer's constant exploitation of the different semantic values of words like "worthy," "gentil," "fair."

To illustrate briefly: the adjective "worthy" is used as the keyword of the Knight's portrait, where it has a profound and serious significance, indicating not only the Knight's social status, but also the ethical qualities appropriate to it. In the Friar's portrait, the word is ironically used to indicate the Friar's lack of these ethical qualities—but it can also be read nonironically, as a reference to social status:

> For unto swich a worthy man as he
> Acorded nat, as by his facultee,
> To have with sike lazars aqueyntaunce.
> It is nat honest, it may nat avaunce,
> For to deelen with no swich poraille.
> (ll. 243–47)

The reference to social status seems to be the only one in the portrait of the Merchant, who "was a worthy man with alle" (l. 283). By the time we reach the Franklin's portrait, the word is used with a vague heartiness which seems to indicate little beside the narrator's approval: "Was nowher swich a worthy vavasour" (l. 360). This attempt to use words with something of the different emphases and connotations that they have in conversation rather than precise and consistent meaning, produces an impression of the complexity of the characters, for it too makes it difficult to pass absolute judgement on them. The shifting meaning given to the vocabulary parrallels, and indeed, helps to produce, the shifting bases from which we approach the characters. And the ambivalence reflects not merely their moral ambiguity, but also our own; the shifting semantic values we give to words reveals in us relative, not absolute, standards for judging people. The characters whose own values are absolute are described in absolute terms; the others inhabit a linguistic realm which is more applicable to our everyday unthinking acceptance of different criteria.

The irony in this wordplay has a more important role than to serve as a comic cloak for moral criticism. Chaucer uses it to raise some very serious questions. For example, in the Knight's portrait, the word "curteisie" is associated with an absolute ideal to which one may devote one's whole life (l. 46). In the literary genre of the *chanson de geste,* from which the Knight seems to have stepped, this ideal provides the whole sphere of reference for action. The Squire's "curteisie" (l. 99), on the other hand, is linked with other characteristics, such as his devotion to love, and his courtly accomplishments, which make it seem not so much an exacting ideal, as part of a way of life for someone who occupies a particular social station. The "curteisie" in which the Prioress "set ful muchel hir lest" (l. 132) should be spiritual courtesy, as we have seen, but it has become in her case embarrassingly worldly; instead of striving to please a heavenly spouse by spiritual grace, she has become the female counterpart of the type represented by the Squire. At the same time as another idealistic and religious meaning of "curteisie" is being evoked, the concrete manifestations of "cheere of court" (ll. 139–40)—personal adornment and accomplished manners—are shown to be in sharp opposition to it. We are left with a sense of the contradictory values implied by the term. Is it a religious value or a secular one? Is it an absolute value, or merely appropriate to a certain social class or age group? Is the refined behaviour involved in the conception to be defined as consideration of others, or as ritualised manners? The different uses of the word reflect not only our shifting attitude to the characters, but also to the ideal itself.

This I take to be the essence of Chaucer's satire; it does not depend on wit and verbal pyrotechnic, but on an attitude which cannot be pinned down, which is always escaping to another view of things and producing comedy from the disparateness between the two. In some cases, the disparateness is indeed that between truth and illusion:

> And over al, *ther as profit sholde arise,*
> Curteis he was, and lowely of servyse.
> (ll. 249–50)

> For he hadde power of confessioun,
> *As seyde hymself,* moore than a curat.
> (ll. 228–29)

The necessity that the illusion should be seen through, should be dispersed, explains why we have the presentation of characters who are by any standards truly admirable, the use of words like "worthy" to indicate moral as well as purely social values, and the use of unpleasant imagery to describe characters who are also morally unpleasant.

But in other instances we are not allowed to disperse the illusion, because we have only suspicions to set against it. What "true" appellation are we to oppose to the description of the Franklin as a "worthy vavasour"? Do we *know* that his feasts are selfish ones from which the poor are excluded? Do we feel his pleasant appearance to be *belied* by his character? And what about the Merchant—"Ther wiste no wight that he was in dette"—and yet we do not know either that his prosperity is a hollow pretence. Or the Reeve—"Ther koude no man brynge him in arrerage"—because he was honest, or because he was skilled at covering up his fraud?

I should say that all these ambiguities, together with the "omission of the victim" and the confusion of moral and emotional reactions, add up to Chaucer's *consistent removal of the possibility of moral judgement*. In other words, our attention is being drawn to the *illusion*; its occasional dispersal is to demonstrate that it is an illusion, but the illusion itself is made into the focal point of interest. A comment of Auerbach on the irony of the *Libro de Buen Amor* of the Archpriest Juan Ruiz enables us to express this in other terms:

> What I have in mind is not so much a conscious irony of the poet, though that too is plentiful, as a kind of objective irony implicit in the candid, untroubled coexistence of the most incompatible things.

The General Prologue leads us to discover in ourselves the coexistence of different methods of judging people, the coexistence of different semantic values, each perfectly valid in its own context, and uses this to suggest the way in which the coexistence of the people themselves is achieved. The social cohesion revealed by the Prologue is not the moral or religious one of Langland's ideal, but the ironic one of the "candid, untroubled coexistence of the most incompatible things."

It is remarkable that many of the methods through which Chaucer achieves this significance for the Prologue are also those through which he persuades us of the individuality of the pilgrims. Thus, important for both irony and "characterisation" in the Prologue is what may be called the lack of context. In estates satire, the estates are not described in order to inform us about their work, but in order to present moral criticism; the removal of this purpose in the Prologue results, as Rosemary Woolf has noted, in the presentation of class failings as if they were personal idiosyncrasies, and thus gives us a sense of the individuality of the figures. Similarly the lack of narrative context, which would provide an apparent motive for mentioning many items of description by giving them storial significance, creates the illusion of factual reporting in the Prologue, which has been convincingly related to Boccaccio's use of this technique in the *Decameron*.

> Gratuituous information . . . creates wonderfully the illusion of factual reporting. What other reason could there be for volunteering such a point if not that it actually happened?

And the illusion of factual reporting in turn aids the creation of irony; there is no obligation to "place" the pilgrims on a moral scale if one is simply reporting on their existence.

Yet the fascination of the actual is not quite the same for Chaucer and Boccaccio. The aim of the Prologue is not to describe human beings in the same spirit as that in which Browning's Fra Lippo Lippi painted people,

> Just as they are, careless of what comes of it
> . . . and count it crime
> To let a truth slip.

In order to show the distinction, the characterisation of the pilgrims may be briefly compared with Chaucer's great achievement in *Troilus and Criseyde:* the characterisation of Criseyde.

Coghill has made a useful distinction between Chaucerian characters who are presented through description, "the selection and adding up of outward detail into the prime number that makes a human being," and those who grow out of speech and action, such as the Host. This distinction can be taken further. Pandarus is a character who grows out of speech and action, but this is almost entirely observed from the outside. We do not see very far into the workings of his mind, and his inward attitude to such an apparently important matter as his own unrequited love affair is left undefined. With Criseyde, on the other hand, we are introduced to the minute-by-minute workings of her mind, to a complex notion of her psychological processes, and to a character subject to the influence of *time*. This development begins at the moment when she is first acquainted with Troilus's love for her, and deliberates on what to do. Her plea to Pandarus to stay, when he is marching out in anger with a threat of suicide because of her first reaction of dismay, proceeds from a whole range of motives—fear, pity, concern for her reputation, the consciousness that she has responded cruelly to what is, on the surface, an innocent request. The significance of the two stanzas in which these turbulent reactions are described lies in their mixed nature. Her responses are both calculating and instinctive, selfish and charitable. No single motive can be isolated as the "true" one.

This is equally true of Criseyde's deliberations, when left alone, on whether to accept Troilus's love. Troilus's high social rank, his handsomeness, his bravery, his intelligence and virtue, his suffering on her behalf, are all admitted as influences, and conversely, fear of unpleasantness, of betrayal, of what people will say (bk. 2, ll. 659–65, 701–28, 771–805). Criseyde is alternately overwhelmed at the honour done to her and conscious that she well deserves it (ll. 735–49). She tries to determine coolly and rationally what will be the best course of action, and is then swayed by a song, a nightingale and a dream (ll. 82ff., 918ff.,925ff.). This is a situation in which the workings of Criseyde's mind tell us more about her than the actual thoughts she entertains. We have an extraordinarily realistic presentation of the complicated responses and decisions of human beings. One further touch is worth noting; in book 4, Criseyde earnestly assures Troilus that the reason for her yielding to him was neither pleasure, his high rank, nor even his bravery, but "moral vertu, grounded upon trouthe" (ll. 1667–73). The fact that we have seen a very different situation in book 2 does not mean that Criseyde is insincere. It is a true statement with regard to the *present*—the time dimension not only alters the character and our view of her, it retrospectively validates her selection of one single aspect of a complex past. There is no single "truth" in the sphere of human motives.

There is no ambiguity of depth of character comparable to this in the Prologue. The state of the Merchant's finances is knowable, although we do not know it, in a way that the state of Criseyde's mind is not knowable. There is some ambiguity of mind indicated by external devices, such as the motto on the Prioress's brooch. But comparison with the characterisation of Criseyde reveals even more clearly that the complexity of the Prologue portraits consists much more in our attitude to them than in their own characteristics. Bronson seems to be saying something like this in claiming that we are much more deeply involved with the narrator than with any of the characters in the General Prologue, "for he is almost the only figure in his 'drama' who is fully realised psychologically and who truly matters to us." The centre of interest in the Prologue is not in any depiction of human character, in actuality for its own sake; it is in our relationship with the actual, the way in which we perceive it and the attitudes we adopt to it, and the narrator stands here for the ambiguities and complexities that characterise this relationship.

If we draw together the results of this discussion, we find that the ethic we have in the Prologue is an ethic of this world. The constant shifting of viewpoints means that it is relativist; in creating our sense of this ethic the estates aspect is of fundamental importance, for it means that in each portrait we have the sense of a specialised way of life. A world of specialised skills, experience, terminology and interests confronts us; we see the world through the eyes of a lazy Monk or a successful Merchant, and simultaneously realise the latent tension between his view and our own. But the tension is latent, because the superficial agreement and approval offered in the ironic comment has this amount of reality—it really reflects the way in which we get on with our neighbours, by tacit approval of the things we really consider wrong, by admiring techniques more than the ends they work towards, by regarding unethical behaviour as amusing as long as the results are not directly unpleasant for us, by adopting, for social reasons, the viewpoint of the person with whom we are associating, and at the same time feeling that his way of life is "not our business."

To say that the General Prologue is based on an ethic of this world is not to adopt the older critical position that Chaucer is unconcerned with morality. The adoption of this ethic at this particular point does not constitute a definitive attitude but a piece of observation—and the comic irony ensures that the reader does not identify with this ethic. Chaucer's inquiry is epistemological as well as moral. This is how the world operates, and as the world, it can operate no other way. The contrast with heavenly values is made at the end of the *Canterbury Tales,* as critics have noted, but it is made in such a way that it cannot affect the validity of the initial statement—the world can only operate by the world's values. One's confidence in seeing this as the movement of the *Canterbury Tales* is increased by the observation that this parallels the movement in *Troilus and Criseyde*: consistent irony throughout the poem, the coexistence of incompatible things, the sharp demonstration of their incompatibility in the Epilogue and yet the tragic consciousness that their coexistence—indeed in the case of *Troilus* their unity—is as inevitable as their incompatibility. And yet the differences between the two works are significant. The narrator in the *Troilus* is led by the conclusion of his story to reject his own—and our—experience of the beauty and nobility of what has gone before. Although we do not accept his Epilogue as the *only* valid response to the experience of the *Troilus,* this emotional rejection plays a large part in establishing the tragic finality of the work. The *Canterbury Tales* do not have the same sort of finality. The "final statement" in the *Tales* comes not from the narrator, but from the Parson, who has not participated as we have in the worlds of the other pilgrims. In rejecting the world of the Miller, for example, he is not rejecting something for which he has felt personal enthusiasm—such as the narrator of the *Troilus* feels at the consummation of the love affair. And *because* the final statement is given to the Parson, the narrator of the *Canterbury Tales* remains an observer who can sympathetically adapt to or report a whole range of experiences and attitudes to them. The relation between the General Prologue and the Parson's Tale is more subtle than a simple opposition between *cupiditas* and *caritas.*

The *Prologue* presents the world in terms of worldly values, which are largely concerned with an assessment of façades, made in the light of half-knowledge, and on the basis of subjective criteria. Subjectivity characterises both the pilgrims' attitude to the world, and the world's (or the reader's) attitude to the pilgrims. But at least in their case, it must be repeated that their views on the world are not individual ones, but are attached to their callings—in medieval terms, their estates. The Prologue proves to be a poem about work. The society it evokes is not a collection of individuals or types with an eternal or universal significance, but particularly a society in which work as a social experience conditions personality and the standpoint from which an individual views the world. In the Prologue, as in history, it is specialised work which ushers in a world where relativised values and the individual consciousness are dominant.

Memory and Form

Donald R. Howard

Memory, central to the experience of reading *The Canterbury Tales,* is embodied in it as its central fiction and becomes the controlling principle of its form. The expressed idea of the work is that the pilgrim Chaucer, like the pilgrim Dante of the *Commedia,* reports an experience of his own which includes stories told by others. Both are returned travellers, both rely on memory. Frances Yates [in *The Art of Memory*] has even suggested that Dante relied for his structuring principles upon the artificial memory systems prevalent in the Middle Ages. This fictional premise, probably Chaucer's greatest debt to Dante, is hardly ever noted. Simple and natural as it seems to us who read novels, it was unusual for a medieval work explicitly to take the form of an imagined feat of memory: we find it in romances, but only a simple version of it. And it was unusual for a work to have as the subject of that memory an imagined experience of the author's own.

It is not surprising that this fundamental fiction of *The Canterbury Tales* has been overlooked. Chaucer the "observer" and "persona" have been fixed in people's minds since Kittredge's day, and these conceptions mitigate the element of personal experience in favor of distance, irony, and control. Chaucer used to be admired as an open-eyed observer of contemporary life (which he was) and so reckoned a naif; it seems astonishing now to find Kittredge in 1914 arguing that "a naif Collector of Customs would be a paradoxical monster." Since then, the sophisticated and ironical Chaucer, adopting for satiric purposes the persona of a naif, has been the going thing in Chaucer criticism. Forty years after Kittredge's lecture, Professor Donaldson in a famous article described this persona, emphasizing the disparity between Chaucer the pilgrim, Chaucer the poet, and Chaucer the man. In a climate of formalism the fictional pilgrim was, and perhaps still is, often viewed as a kind of puppet; but in fact, Donaldson closed his article by pointing to the relatedness of pilgrim and man, doubting that one can tell which has the last word. Among those interested in the rhetoric of fiction or the "dynamics" of literature, this interrelation of man and persona has captured some amount of interest; where it was once possible to talk seriously about the "finiteness of the narrator-role," such a phrase now seems all gesture and bluster. Not that role-playing isn't involved; but in all role-playing, masquerade, or disguise, the art and excitement come from the living presence of the performer behind the role or mask.

The remarkable aspect of this performer's mind, as he presents it to us, is not just a power of observation but a prodigious memory. Memory is endemic to all storytelling and all literary composition; Mnemosyne, we recall, was the mother of the Muses. St. Augustine in an amazing passage showed how memory is endemic to understanding itself:

> I carry . . . facts in my memory, and I also remember how I learned them. I have also heard, and remember, many false arguments put forward to dispute them. Even if the arguments are false, the fact that I remember them is not false. I also remember distinguishing between the true facts and the false theories advanced against them, and there is a difference between seeing myself make this distinction now and remembering that I have made it often in the past, every time that I have given the matter any thought. So I not only remember that I have often understood these facts in the past, but I also commit to memory the fact that I understand them and distinguish the truth from the falsehood at the present moment. By this means I ensure that later on I shall remember that I understood them at this time. And I remember that I have remembered, just as later on, if I remember that I have been able to remember these facts now, it will be by the power of my memory that I shall remember doing so.
>
> (*Confessions*, trans. R. S. Pine-Coffin)

Augustine recognized that memory contains all experience, even the experience of forgetting. For all that happens to us in time there must be memory. Every writer, as he composes, must remember what he has set out to write and what he has already written—the action is divided, as Augustine says of recitations, between memory and expectation until all has "passed into the province of memory." Durations themselves cannot be known without memory, so even language depends on memory, requiring the recollection of syllables spoken in sequence and the measurement of long and short vowels. But this reliance of storytelling and composition on memory rarely used to be brought into literary works themselves. Medieval writers were more apt to write as if authority resided in them, so that the "I" in medieval works is frequently impersonal. At other times they wrote as recorders or copyists—Chaucer adopts this pose in the *Troilus*—putting into their books what they found in others. Dante in the *Vita Nuova* does claim to be writing of personal experience from memory, but he depicts memory as a "book" and himself as a copyist and glossator of that book. Even bards, minstrels, or scops, among whom prodigious feats of memory *were* performed, rarely alluded to memory itself. The fashionable premise of fictions in Chaucer's time was the dream, and Chaucer's early poems all employ that convention; but little was ever made of the fact that the dream is remembered, and little notice given to the act of writing it down. When Chaucer ended *The Book of the Duchess* with a specific reference to the act of writing the dream in verse, he was doing something unusual, and even here he made nothing of memory as the step between dreaming and writing: he saw that step as a matter of time moving on in "process." The dreamer hears a clock strike twelve, wakes, finds the book he had been reading when he dropped off, and says,

> Thought I, "This is so queint a sweven
> That I wol, by process of time,
> Fonde to put this sweven in ryme
> As I can best, and that anon."
> This was my sweven; now hit is don.
>
> (ll. 1330–34)

The narrator of *The Canterbury Tales,* like the narrator of *The Book of the Duchess,* remembers a past experience well enough to write it down in detail—to describe some twenty-nine pilgrims and repeat in their own words the tales they told. His memory becomes a wellspring of narrative, like the "old book" in the *Troilus*. This fictional tour de force of memory makes *The Canterbury Tales* different from other frame narratives. It was how Chaucer bestowed upon his work the ironic and equivocal stamp which no such work had had before: every pilgrim and every tale stands out as an independent reality but all is mediated by the author-narrator. If he got the hint anywhere, he got it from Dante, or the dream-vision, or some actual account of a pilgrimage. No writer of a frame narrative had done anything like it. Boccaccio, in neither the *Filocolo,* the *Ameto,* or the *Decameron,* used the first person and never claimed directly to have participated in the framing action; one has to know the code name "Filostrato" to get the implication that the author was present among the company and even at that his point of view does not color what he reports. Sercambi, though present on the journey, told all the tales himself and referred to himself in the third person. In Gower's *Confessio Amantis,* most like *The Canterbury Tales* in subject matter, themes, conventions, and motifs, we get the faceless "I" of medieval complaint who identifies himself as the writer, and the conventional love-vision (not explicitly a dream); the tales are told in Boethian fashion by the Lover and his confessor Genius; the organizing principle is that of the "tree of vices." In Chaucer we find a form, simple and natural though it seems six centuries later, which was then new: the voice of the poet himself recalls the re-creates the voices of others, the form and matter seeming to take shape as they come into mind.

This last remark will delay us a moment, for the way things come into mind has changed since Chaucer's time. The physiology of memory is no doubt basically the same in each individual, but things remembered vary with the importance placed upon them by individuals or cultures, and the character of memory itself varies with our notions of what memory is and does. Because Freud or Wordsworth placed more importance on childhood memories, they likely had more childhood memories (though of very different kinds). Preconceptions about history, or causality, or human nature doubtless affect the selection, association, and structuring of memory. If we are to see *The Canterbury Tales* as a fictional feat of memory, then, we have to ask whether memory itself did not have a different character in the fourteenth century from what it has now.

As with most other things, the medievals had two contradictory notions of memory and believed in both. From one point of view they saw memory as a "faculty" of the soul and forgetfulness as its failure to function well. Memory played a minor role in the life of the mind. It was one of the five "inner senses" or "inward wits" (with common sense, fantasy, imagination, and the "estimative" sense) which resided in the sensitive soul. Among the powers of the soul this sensitive power was higher than the vegetative but inferior to the locomotive and the intellectual. That memory contained all experience, a fact Augustine marvelled at, did not raise its status much; Augustine was arguing, after all, that we must seek God beyond memory or through the total experience of memory, but not in particular memories. Memory was supplied by imagination, the image-making faculty of the mind, which extrapolated "phantasms" from the evidence of the senses and could make combinations of these phantasms. Because memory was a storehouse of such images, it was bound to the intense particularities of the sensible world, which made it the less reliable as a means of knowing truth. Memory was "an organ, a cerebral ventricle," and "what is described in it must be something sensible, which has all the limitations of individuality and particular nature." Such an estimate of memory, fostered by the old faculty psychology, lingered into the seventeenth century. Modern conceptions of associative process, of a form-giving or structuring power inherent in memory itself, were foreign to the medievals. They saw memory as a storehouse on which one must *impose* form. Thus Augustine refers to the "compartments" of memory. St. Thomas adds that memory stores intentions as well as images. When Chaucer the pilgrim claims to remember the particularities of a past experience he is not therefore boasting of mental powers which were admired or thought reliable. He is limiting his scope to the experience of the temporal or secular world.

But while medieval thinkers put a low value on memory when they saw it as a faculty of the soul, they valued it highly as a necessity of everyday life. St. Augustine, with his customary verbal felicity, called it the "stomach of the mind." From this practical view they imagined memory had to be supplied with shelves, so to speak, and kept in order. They could hardly do otherwise in an age before the printing press when books were scarce and paper dear, and when devices used to write memoranda on, like wax tablets, were cumbersome. One always supposed men had better memories in those days; but it was not until Frances Yates published her remarkable book, *The Art of Memory*, that most of us realized how fully men *trained* their memories. The memory systems of the ancient world, Miss Yates shows, survived into the Middle Ages; there is even a short treatise *De arte memorativa* by Chaucer's contemporary Bishop Bradwardine. This "artificial" memory was understood as a corrective to human ignorance, a way of supplying capacities the mind had lost because of the Fall. Its moral utility was comparable to the fact that a remembered image carries with it an "intention" (for example, that the wolf is dangerous); but associating intelligible ideas with images was an art which had to be learned. It was useful as a means of remembering moral truths—the "tree of virtues and vices" familiar to any student of the Middle Ages were almost certainly memory devices; Miss Yates even argues with some conviction that the scrulptures in Gothic cathedrals were influenced by and even intended as memory devices. But apart from this moralizing use of artificial memory, it was a practical necessity; it was, we know, taught as a phase of rhetoric, and beyond a doubt it was used for quotidian purposes in place of the maps, directories, and lists which have become second nature in the modern world.

Artificial memory worked on the principles of order and association. It was by nature spatial and visual. It required, first, a mental store of "places"—mental pictures of actual buildings or interiors. To these one associated mnemonic images or sometimes words, "placing" one upon a column, another on an altar, another in an alcove; visual images were thought more useful than words. Meditate for a moment on this habit of mind and one becomes aware of the most startling difference between our medieval ancestors and ourselves. We memorize a few things—grammatical forms, or the presidents of the United States, or the English kings—almost always in lists and with words; otherwise the memory of modern man is an intellectual rabbit's warren made from slips of paper. But the medievals made of their memories vast storehouses of visual images, disposed upon structured "places," systematized and concrete.

That Chaucer knew an artificial memory system there can be no doubt. If, as most people now believe, he was educated at the Inns of Court, he would have been required to get by memory vast amounts of legal information. We learn in the General Prologue about the Man of Law that "every statute koude he plein by rote" and that he had "in termes" all the cases and judgments since King William's time. Anyone holding the kind of posts Chaucer held would have needed to remember laws and names and people and a myriad of facts. Besides, he *thought* of memory as a storehouse: while he uses the reflexive form ("remember me") or the impersonal one ("it remembereth me"), he often uses such idioms as "to have in memory" or "have remembrance," "to draw to memory," "to clepe agein unto memory" to "fall, be, or put" in remembrance. These usages suggest control over a disciplined memory and represent memory as a *place* supplied at will by a storehouse; implicit in them are the habits of "artificial" memory—order, association, and visualization.

Memory is, moreover, central to the reading experience which *The Canterbury Tales* affords: as we come to each new tale we must call to mind from the General Prologue the description of the pilgrim telling it; if we do not, a whole level of meaning drops away. This is, everyone knows, one of the notably original elements of *The Canterbury Tales:* the tales themselves characterize the tellers and so contribute to the narrative of the pilgrimage itself. If it is true that Chaucer read the work aloud at court, his audience could not have kept the left index finger stuck in the General Prologue, as we do, at the beginning of each tale. They would have had to recall "the condicioun / Of each of hem. . . . And which they weren, and of what degree, / And eek in what array that they were inne." If they could not do this, their memories would have had to be refreshed from time to time, or they would have had to miss an exciting feature of the work. Sometimes the headlinks, prologues, and tales themselves remind us of the pilgrim's traits as set forth in the General Prologue, but this is not always so. True, the tales facinate in themselves. But the unity of conception which distinguishes *The Canterbury Tales* in its fullest complexity relies on memory or the refreshing of memory: it presupposes a listener who can remember the pilgrims or a reader who can turn over the leaves.

The narrator claims to be remembering the pilgrims, and seems to be describing them as he first encountered them at the inn; that is the setting, at the moment when he launches into the description—"ere that I ferther in this tale pace." Yet as he describes them he includes details about their appearance on the road and even details about their private lives at home. Though he claims to be an objective reporter, he turns out strangely omniscient—a fact sometimes put forth as evidence against the "realism" of the General Prologue, which it is. If we ask "where we are" as we read the General Prologue, the answer must be neither on the road nor in the inn, but in the realm of mental images, of memory, of hearsay and surmise, of empathy, even of fantasy. And Chaucer draws attention to himself fictionalized as observer and recorder; we relate to him, and his participation in the pilgrimage becomes part of the fictional reality. We pass through the looking glass of the narrator's mind into the remembered world of the pilgrimage; from it into the remembered worlds of the various pilgrims; and from these sometimes even into the remembered worlds of their characters.

This controlled lapse from one remembered world to another, this regression by successive steps into the past and the unreal, is the essential principle of form in *The Canterbury Tales*. The General Prologue which introduces it is structured upon principles of memory as memory was then experienced; and it introduces principles of form and structure which are to operate in the work as a whole. Its memory structure is comprised of several components superimposed, and these we shall see best by separating them into the features of association and order which they owe to the habit of artificial memory.

The characters are arranged in associations easiest to remember, associations of class, alliance, and dependency endemic to medieval society.

First, they are arranged according to the conception of the Three Estates. There is the aristocracy (Knight and Squire, with their Yeoman); then the clergy (the Prioress and her entourage, the Monk and the Friar); all the rest, from the Merchant on, belong to the "commons," except for the Clerk and Parson whom I shall mention in a moment, and except for the Summoner and Pardoner, two classless pariahs who are put at the end. This perfectly natural order is then subdivided—Chaucer might well have had in mind Geoffrey of Vinsauf's advice, that one should divide a thing to be remembered into small parts. He arranges the pilgrims in associations so natural that because of them the people themselves in such relationships would have fallen into groups in the inn or on the road, and we are told they did so. There is the Knight, his son, and their yeoman; the Prioress, her companion and "preestes three"; the Man of Law and the Franklin; the five Guildsmen and their cook; the Parson and his brother the Plowman; the Summoner and Pardoner. Call to mind any of these and their companions come to mind automatically. Others are described together, though we are not told they travelled together: the Monk and Friar (two kinds of religious); the Shipman, Physician, and Wife (three "bourgeois"); the Miller, Manciple, and Reeve (three small-fry functionaries).

The well-known "idealized" portraits seem thrown into this order at random. Three of them (Knight, Parson, and Plowman) correspond to the Three Estates. The portrait of the Clerk is idealized too, and perhaps he represents a style of life (that of the universities, or of humanism) which Chaucer considered separate from the usual three. But the Clerk comes for no apparent reason between the Merchant and the Man of Law, the Parson and Plowman for no apparent reason between the Wife and Miller. I should like to offer a possible explanation for this seemingly haphazard arrangement. If we take the description of the Prioress and her followers and that of the Guildmen and their cook as single descriptions (which they are), and if we count the description of the Host, the portraits of the General Prologue can then be seen arranged symmetrically into three groups of seven, each headed by an ideal portrait:

Knight:	Squire, Yeoman, Prioress, Monk, Friar, Merchant
Clerk:	Man of Law, Franklin, Guildsmen, Shipman, Physician, Wife
Parson, Plowman:	Miller, Manciple, Reeve, Summoner, Pardoner, Host

I do not mean to suggest that this arrangement is like statues in niches or an allegorical painting, but it is interesting that the "images" in artificial memory *were* emblematic or symbolical, that is, were meant to call abstractions to mind. To the medievals, as Frances Yates points out, memory's highest function was to remember moral precepts. The "ideal" portraits undeniably have an emblematic quality, and the other portraits, for all their warts and red stockings—which make them memorable—suggest, in the old phrase, "types of society." Yet one of the principles of artificial memory was that one remembered best the image which startled one's feelings. Hence the mixture of particularities and abstractions which we admire in the General Prologue was itself a phase of artificial memory; as Geoffrey of Vinsauf said, "delight alone makes the faculty of memory strong." Then, too, the symmetry of the arrangement is characteristically medieval; some might suspect numerical composition or number symbolism clicking away in the background. Such efforts at proportionableness were a habit of mind in the Middle Ages, and the ordered "places" of artificial memory gave powerful support to such a habit if they did not create it. I think Chaucer apportioned the ideal portraits in this architectonic way more by habit than design; it is not really an effective aide-mémoire. But it results in an arbitrary shape or placement which resembles the artificial order imposed as an aid to memory upon words or things by "placing" them upon the doors or columns or windows which one had imprinted in one's mind for such a purpose.

What is the idea behind such an arrangement? What purpose does it serve? Chaucer was straining at many purposes—to group the pilgrims in associations reflecting fourteenth-century society which would be easily remembered; to marshal them according to the prized concept of the Three Estates which his friend Gower had used with such brittle certainty; to include ideals of conduct among his satirical vignettes; to get order into the series, an order based on what mattered most to most of the pilgrims, status and money. The kinds of order we perceive in this complex arrangement leave some loose ends, but each detail has a rightness of its own. The Parson and Plowman are put together because they are "brothers"—which suggests an ideal relationship between clergy and commons. The idealized Clerk represents an estate other than the traditional three, but by Chaucer's time the universities *were* a world unto themselves. The Host, being the leader, is appropriately described apart from the series and last. And the Merchant is, lonely man, between the Friar and the Clerk where no one in the world would expect him to be. (The placement, though, is suggestive. The Merchant introduces a group of bourgeois, i.e., members of the "merchant class." The Clerk comes next, then the Man of Law and Franklin. A series of contrasts is involved—the Friar's and Merchant's kinds of venality, the Merchant's venality and the Clerk's unworldliness, the Clerk's use of his learning and the Lawyer's use of his, and so on. . . . It is notable that the Merchant's tale follows the Clerk's, answering its idealism with disillusionment.)

So much else is accomplished in this arrangement that it is remarkable it all hangs together as perfectly as it does. The "voice" is introduced first as the poet's (ll. 1–18; line numbers conform with F. N. Robinson, 2d ed.), then as the pilgrim's or returned traveller's. There is a kind of progression in the gravity of the pilgrims' shortcomings: we get first the pleasant self-indulgence of the Squire, then the minor peccadillos of the Prioress and the abuses of the Monk, the various swindling of the burghers and churls, and at length the monstrous exploitations of the Summoner and Pardoner. Because the narrator's wide-eyed delight in all these sorts and conditions of men and women is so unswerving, the irony becomes greater as their vices become more serious. After the aristocracy and clergy are introduced, a bevy of "commons" is paraded in what seems no particular order; it is perhaps true that the pilgrims are introduced in a socioeconomic schema based on the degree of respectability with which they earn their livings (but I can see no socioeconomic reason why the Merchant precedes the eminent Man of Law, and no explanation for the sequence Guildsmen-Shipman-Physician-Wife). In a general way, the "commons" are all independent entrepreneurs; those in a servile or dependent state (Yeoman, Cook, Plowman) are introduced with those on whom they depend; and the last group (Miller, Manciple, Reeve, Summoner, Pardoner) are lower in status, more given to swindling, and fonder of fabliaux.

This arrangement in all its ramifications neatly mirrors the conditions of fourteenth-century society which, like all societies, was stratified. Knights and clerks were easily distinguished by their titles and tonsures. There were serfs still, though there are none on this pilgrimage. The "commons" were more subtly stratified—they were not really disposed into a class or even classes but into numerous gradations. The "class structure" in the fourteenth century was conceived of as a hierarchy, and like all social structures *was* a hierarchy; but it was changing and mobile. "Middle" classes existed, though the *conception* "middle class" did not. The "Three Estates" was an established authoritative idea, but it did not interfere with practical distinctions of prestige, which had many minute degrees. A man of the fourteenth century might in his mind have lumped into one "estate" the Franklin, the Physician, and the Miller, but he would readily have known which should go through a door first.

The General Prologue, then, as everyone always says, introduces a cross-section of fourteenth-century English society. It used to be styled a "portrait gallery," but if it is like that at all it is like a remembered portrait gallery, the figures themselves marshalled in convenient mnemonic groups which correspond to actualities and probabilities of fourteenth-century life, symmetrically disposed as if on mnemonic "places." We will understand the General Prologue best if we discard all notions of a serial description. If descriptions seriatim were all he wanted, Chaucer would have been well advised to parcel out the portraits among the tales. He described instead a *group*. Like any group it is made of individuals, but it has a dynamics of its own based on interpersonal and social relationships. Like any group, it is a society in little. The group behaves in a predictable way: they gather into subgroups based on social degrees and small-group solidarity—those of a household or a retinue or guild, those with similar professions or trades, stick together. A leader emerges, and the group becomes a "flock." A game-like aura pervades the arrangements: those superior in class to the Host assent to his leadership, but the Host is exceedingly deferential to them and makes an effort to observe accepted social proprieties. As in any group those who violate the norms are made pariahs: this is so of the Summoner and especially of the Pardoner. As the pilgrimage progresses, hostilities break out which are based on cultural or temperamental conflicts. Opinion leaders emerge—the Host because he has charisma, the Knight because he has status. The group gangs up on some, takes sides with others: the Pardoner is made a scapegoat in part with his own collaboration, the drunken Cook becomes the butt of a cruel joke. Disagreements and discussions arise, and a spirit of competitiveness emerges—in telling tales the pilgrims are often moved to "quit" one another.

I hope no one will suppose that in saying the General Prologue reflects a contemporary society and group dynamics I am suggesting that Chaucer broke with literary conventions and went "direct to life." It is quite the contrary; he used literary conventions as a means of interpreting life. For the conception of a journey remembered by a returned traveller he was indebted to Dante and to accounts of journeys and pilgrimages like Mandeville's *Travels*. For its "mentalistic" form, its quality of inner, remembered experience, the design of the General Prologue and of *The Canterbury Tales* was indebted to the French dream-vision. The correspondence between *The Canterbury Tales*, the *Roman*, Gower's *Confessio Amantis*, and Chaucer's four early dream-visions is palpable: each begins with a description of a particular season, introduces a narrator, describes a place, introduces a company of personages depicted in panel fashion, singles out a leader or guide, and proposes a device which orders the remainder of the poem. Let me add that Chaucer had already tried out in his dream-visions those individual variations on the pattern which taken together make *The Canterbury Tales* unique: in *The Book of the Duchess* he depicted a real memory, the haunting memory of the Duchess Blanche; in *The Legend of Good Women* he introduced a series of narratives; and in *The Parliament of Fowls* he represented spirited dialogue among characters from different social strata.

The General Prologue is then a natural evolution from the dream vision with memory replacing dream. It is like a *vade mecum* which we must carry with us as we proceed into the tales. It informs the whole; it centers attention upon the artist-narrator's consciousness as essential to the conception of the whole, and makes us aware that in consciousness things remembered are by nature things of this world. The General Prologue is therefore above all what gives unity to the whole. In constructing his work this way Chaucer followed Geoffrey of Vinsauf's advice perfectly: "Let the mind's inner compass," said Geoffrey, "first circumscribe the entire area of the subject matter." The General Prologue in a number of ways reveals and imposes principles of unity upon the tales that follow:

> The General Prologue *seems* to have a random lack of organization, but is artfully structured to reveal a typifying group. The tales *seem* to follow spontaneously, but many are artfully ordered into thematic or dramatic clusters.
>
> The General Prologue includes ideal figures at fixed though seemingly random intervals. The tales include ideal narratives—the tales of Constance, Griselda, Virginia, Cecilia—dispersed among the tales or clusters of tales.
>
> In the General Prologue, the Host dominates the group and is the leader. In the tales he directs their order when he can.
>
> In the General Prologue we get elements of class conflict, conflict of interest, and temperamental differences. In the tales these produce moments of competition and aggression which account for the order of most other tales.
>
> In the General Prologue, the very first thing mentioned after the season is the pilgrimage to Jerusalem (in the allusion to "palmers" and "straunge strondes"). In the Parson's Prologue we are reminded of the glorious pilgrimage to Jerusalem celestial.
>
> In the General Prologue the narrator's feat of memory is announced and begun. In the tales it opens to us a world of remembered fictions, the irrepressible world of story, passed by

books or traditions to the pilgrims, by them to the author-narrator, and by him to us.

In the General Prologue the narrator thus brings the pilgrims into the present through memory, and the Host invites them to tell "Of aventures that whilom have bifalle"; in their tales each, recaptured from the past, recaptures some part of the past. Literary tradition, notable to the point of exaggeration in the opening lines of the General Prologue, becomes the substance of the work: things remembered, known to the mind and spirit, and preserved in language, are the world of *The Canterbury Tales*—a world more real, more articulate, and more perdurable than the day-to-day world, the pilgrimage of human life, which purports to be its subject. At the end we get a prose meditation about the way to deal with that day-to-day world, and after it a terse statement in which the author rejects that world, and with it his books about that world, and "many another book, if they were in my remembrance," to embrace the world he believed existed beyond memory.

Where in all of literature is there any comparable conception? There are other medieval prologues which introduce the form and themes of the work to follow—those of *Piers Plowman* or Gower's *Confessio,* for example, or the *Decameron*—but none is so rich or complex, so totally unified a conception. The opening of *Paradise Lost* or the first book of *The Ring and the Book* may be comparable, but the most instructive comparison is the "Overture" with which Proust began *A la recherche du temps perdu*. In it the characters, the circumstances, the social structure of the day, the character of the narrator's mind, the form of the whole and its major themes are introduced. Everything that is to follow harkens back to this passage—the whole cannot be read without it, because it imposes unity; like *The Canterbury Tales* it even permits us to read sections out of order, to "choose another tale," without losing our awareness of its formal integrity. Proust said the opening of the first novel was written on the same day as the ending of the last, that the whole was a unified idea; who can doubt it? And memory is the principle of form in Proust's work as in Chaucer's.

The differences are even more instructive than the similarities. Proust used an associationist conception of memory, and so centered remembrance wholly upon his own experience. Chaucer used the medieval conceptions of memory as a faculty which stores images and intentions and as an artificial skill by which one stores intelligible ideas; and so he centered remembrance on the structure of a game played along a road and called upon the memories of others, upon tradition. In Proust, memory is involuntary: try as he will

"Marcel" cannot bring back a forgotten world until he gives up trying, then as if by accident a taste and smell bring to mind a structure of associated percepts—a remembered world opens before him. In Chaucer, memory is voluntary: the narrator will do his best to recall "everich a word" and will set out the cast of characters not as they spring from his own inner experience but as they exist in the social world which he shares with his audience. And in the end that memory of a pilgrimage must be allowed to pass out of mind, to take its place among all past things and all forgotten books in the ordered rightness of a transcendent realm. For Proust, writing at the end of the nineteenth and the beginning of the twentieth century, no such ending was possible. He must turn to the world of art itself, must ruminate upon his own accomplishment as part of the human enterprise which creates an order higher than that of things past: a past recaptured and made meaningful by language, by art. Proust gives full and articulate expression to an idea of which Chaucer, living in the dawn of literary humanism, could scarcely have had more than a glimmer. Boccaccio's storytellers, in the *Decameron,* in their elegant, temporary retreat, come closer to it. Yet it is not wholly absent from *The Canterbury Tales,* for we sense the importance which Chaucer, like Proust, attached to the great enterprise of making a book.

History and Form in the General Prologue to the *Canterbury Tales*

Loy D. Martin

Is the form of the General Prologue to the *Canterbury Tales* new or old? Critical sentiment seems on the whole to favor newness; yet there has always remained a sense of craftsmanship and conventionality about the poem which continually reinvigorates the search for a strong antecedent genre. In recent years, a few attempts have been persuasive, notably J. V. Cunningham's structural analysis of the Prologue as a dream vision. Cunningham begins with the assumption that there *must be* an available generic "tradition" which functions intact to shape a poet's experience into poetry, but even his most convinced reader must wonder why Chaucer's use of that tradition escaped notice until the twentieth century. I think this suggests that Cunningham's ideal notions of tradition and genre cause him to overstate his case, but I also think there are very good reasons why he perceived such a strong affinity between the Prologue and the form of the dream vision. In order to save his valuable intuition, then, while offering an alternative set of assumptions about genre formation, I should like to turn briefly to an idea offered by Alastair Fowler in an essay called "The Life and Death of Literary Forms."

Fowler notices that genres, after complex developments in time, often do not simply disappear. Rather they break up into what he calls "modes," methods of writing, like satiric language, which are still recognizable but which can no longer account for the formal properties of entire works. This is a very simple and useful observation; it is undoubtedly true. The question

From *ELH* 45, no. 1 (Spring 1978). © 1978 by the Johns Hopkins University Press, Baltimore/London.

that Fowler does not address is whether genres can appear as well as disappear in this way, whether new genres can sometimes be recognized as expansions of previous "modes" as modes can be recognized as diminutions of previous genres. This seems to me likely and provides a framework in which to identify an historical relationship between the form of the General Prologue and a rhetorical device which appears in, but does not generically constitute, the dream vision poems.

The particular stylistic fragment I have in mind is the rhetorical catalogue of types, which appears frequently in Chaucer's earlier dream vision poems. It not only appears there, it develops, and my very simple argument here will be that it develops finally into the main organizing principle of the General Prologue. I would begin, therefore, by submitting a catalogue from the *Parlement of Foules,* one which seems merely to list the species of trees that the dreamer sees:

> The byldere ok, and ek the hardy asshe;
> The piler elm, the cofre unto carayne;
> The boxtre pipere, holm to whippes lashe;
> The saylynge fyr; the cipresse, deth to playne;
> The shetere ew; the asp for shaftes pleyne;
> The olyve of pes, and eke the dronke vyne;
> The victor palm, the laurer to devyne.

Cataloguing, as Cunningham implies, is central to the dream vision, and even in a simple case like this one, analysis will show us why. Each tree is named by a practical use or a practical problem it presents in the familiar world; they appear in a dream, and, what is most important, they appear in a garden which is immediately represented as timeless. Birds sing the eternal harmony of angelic music, there are no fluctuations of hot and cold, men may not "waxe sek ne old," and day never changes into night. Change, in other words, is explicitly excluded as a normal condition of existence in this garden. Therefore, the temporal functions of the trees are, for the most part, inapplicable. They will not be cut down for their uses because those uses have meaning only in a world in which time rules with implications that are irrelevant here. In the garden, there is no need for shelter and no need to build, no need for coffins because there is no "carayne," no need for pipes because the perfect music of heaven emanates from nature; birdsong and the wind in the living arboreal "instruments." There is no need to sail, no reason to cut and plane boards, and "the shetere ew; the asp for shaftes pleyne" are not useful because there is no war or strife. Thus, there is no need to make peace or celebrate victory, and there is no need to "devyne" the future, because time does not imply change. What seems a simple list of observed trees, then, on second glance, displays a most peculiar structure of irrelevance. Why is this so?

I would argue that, through the dream vision, Chaucer is trying to project a realm of experience or knowledge which transcends some of the obvious limitations of life in time without aspiring to the perfect timelessness of eternity. The trees ornament a timeless realm, and yet their differentiation into species and mundane uses links them irrevocably to the sublunary world. We cannot dismiss the contradiction; we can only say that Chaucer has conceived of his garden as something ambiguously *medium aeternitatem et tempus*. The point of positing such a realm emerges as the poem unfolds and the garden's initial timelessness is revised. The birds abandon their heavenly music for the unregulated "noyse" of debate. Change, strife, and, by implication, death are introduced into what at first appeared to be an eternal paradise. Then, just when the garden world seems indistinguishable from the self-consuming world of men, Nature imposes a solution to the debate and thus effects a partial recovery. The recovery is partial because it restores only that intermediate realm which the catalogue of the trees suggested; it does not restore an ideal paradise. The birds can sing again, but their recovery is not complete: they do not sing the music of the heavenly harmony but a song that "imaked was in Fraunce." The birds' rondeau compromises between the chaos of ear-shattering discord and the music of the spheres. And as the mating ritual resumes its pattern of recurrence "from yer to yeere" in Nature's garden, the concept of cyclic or repetitional time resolves the antithesis between linear time and timelessness, between fatal displacement and perfect stasis. This is, in part, why "commun profit" is invoked in the preservation of the ceremony that enables procreation. Individual birds will die, but the species, through regeneration, will be deathless.

The *Parlement* is a poem that celebrates the resolution of severe polarities, and the rhetorical catalogue is but one technique among many for imagining a mode of knowledge or experience which transcends the strict Augustinian dualism of time and eternity. Moreover, the need for such a projection is central throughout Chaucer's early poems. His ongoing meditation on cyclic repetition testifies to that need, and so does his postulation of extraordinary human experiences which remove the individual briefly from time and allow for a special learning experience. In its most graphic manifestations, this removal involves defining a special place which is neither heaven nor earth. Affrycan takes Scipio to such a place; looking one way, Scipio sees Carthage whole as he could not while earth-bound; looking the other way, he is shown the "Galaxye" and the nine spheres. And he hears "the melodye . . . That cometh of thilke speres thryes thre." The eagle in the *Hous of Fame* plucks the dreamer to a place which is half way between heaven and earth (ll. 713–15) and introduces him to a goddess whose feet rest on earth and whose head is in heaven (ll. 1372–76). Furthermore, these transportations normally occur in dreams, suggesting that the dream vision itself is to be interpreted as a partial transcendence of time. As early as the *Book of the Duchess,* sleep and dreaming function as mediators between life and death, and this notion of an intermediate realm is carried over, without the actual dream, in Troilus's perplexing pause at the eighth sphere as he leaves this life.

In the *Parlement,* the dream vision validates the idea of a garden which seems timeless in some details yet earth-bound in others. I wish to propose that the Canterbury pilgrimage displays a similar ambiguity and that Chaucer, in the General Prologue, abandons the dream and expands the catalogue technique to signify a profound if brief and partial departure from ordinary life. This view will help explain the Prologue's affinity with the dream visions without identifying it with them generically. Thus, in order to see why I wish to assert the Prologue's lineal descent from the simpler catalogue, let us turn to the Canterbury pilgrimage in detail.

The Prologue begins, as we all know, by describing the pilgrimage as a typical event recurring each year in spring, the time of natural and spiritual regeneration—much as the fowls' ritual of mate-choosing recurs annually on St. Valentine's Day in the *Parlement*. People who go on pilgrimages seek "straunge strondes;" they travel to shrines far away from home "in sondry londes." The concept, in other words, which orders Chaucer's account of the custom of the time is that of persons leaving their homes, the locations of their daily lives, to meet in a place which is "straunge," somehow apart from their accustomed environments.

The poet reports that "in that seson on a day" he joined such a group of pilgrims at the Tabard, and he proceeds to describe them in his famous series of portraits. Immediately, in the portrait of the Knight, we can begin to see why we must understand this series in terms of a contrast between pilgrimage and daily life. We first learn of the Knight's personal history. He is a great and honorable soldier and a gracious courtier, and he has fought for his lord in many great battles. Those conflicts, moreover, are specifically named; his fifteen mortal battles Chaucer dwells upon at length. Before relating a single detail of his appearance on the occasion of the pilgrimage, the narrator insistently engages our attention with a life of danger and strife, toil and death. And when description finally follows, it relates that life to the present occasion:

But, for to tellen yow of his array,
His hors were good, but he was nat gay.
Of fustian he wered a gypon
Al bismotered with his habergeon,
For he was late ycome from his viage,
And wente for to doon his pilgrymage.
(1.73–78; F. N. Robinson, 2d ed.)

We have been apprised of that active, worldly life in order that we might know the nature of what the Knight has *left behind* in joining the travelers. His garments show the wear and debris of battle, but he has moved away from his accustomed occupation to share another kind of experience with men and women of the widest possible variety of vocations, social ranks and conditions. The relation of the person to his complex of physical attributes in the Knight's portrait is identical to the relation of noun to modifying phrase or adjective for each tree in the catalogue I discussed earlier. The person (noun) is located in an unaccustomed place (semantic context), and his (its) attributes (modifiers) denote a normal function which is irrelevant to that place or context. The difference is that, in the General Prologue, this rudimentary grammar has been expanded and enriched to become a principle of narrative structure.

I would suggest that the entire series of portraits represents an astonishing realization of the potential of the Chaucerian catalogue as we find it incidentally in the earlier poems. Chaucer introduces all of the pilgrims, as he does the Knight, by relating the nature of their lives and professions. As in the catalogue of birds in the *Parlement,* most are given moral as well as physical attributes, and several, like the Squire, the Merchant, the Clerk, the Shipman, the Wife of Bath, the Reeve, and the Pardoner, are associated with specific locations in keeping with the initial assertion that persons from all over England come together for pilgrimages. Furthermore, the detail which Chaucer devotes to his accounts of the normal life of each pilgrim serves, by implication, to emphasize the departure from those lives represented by the pilgrimage itself. For a fair number of pilgrims, this sense of separation between what they usually do and what they are doing now remains implicit; such is the case with the Squire, the Friar, the Man of Law, the Merchant, the Franklin, and several others. For another group, however, more explicit techniques, some of which we have already encountered in the portrait of the Knight, reenforce our understanding. Like the Knight, a number of pilgrims carry, as part of their "array," implements or other physical attributes which easily identify their worldly occupations but which have no relevance to the context of pilgrimage. Consider, for example, the Yeoman:

> And he was clad in cote and hood of grene.
> A sheef of pecok arwes, bright and kene,
> Under his belt he bar full thriftily,
> (Wel koude he dresse his takel yemanly:
> His armes drouped noght with fetheres lowe)
> And in his hand he baar a myghty bowe.
> A not heed hadde he, with a broun visage.
> (1.103–9)

As the Knight bears on his clothes the evidence of recent battles, the Yeoman, with his "broun visage," leaves no doubt that he has lately come from the exercise of his worldly vocation, one in which the woodsman's skin is darkened by the sun. And he brings the tools of his trade with him, the bow and "yemanly" dressed arrows which see daily use but which clearly have nothing to do with the activity their owner is about to engage in. The same attribute of a deeply tanned face appears in the portrait of the shipman, despite the fact that the "hoote somer" could hardly have "maad his hewe al broun" in April. And that pilgrim is chiefly distinguished by his skill in navigation, a talent which, however indispensable in the world of tempests and treacherous passages, can be of no more use on the road to Canterbury than masts and sails in a timeless garden. Like the Yeoman, moreover, the Haberdasher, Carpenter, Weaver, Dyer, and Tapestry Maker carry with them, to no apparent purpose, the appointed "geere" of their professions. In fact, most of the pilgrims are dressed not explicitly for travel but according to their respective callings.

The Monk will serve to introduce us to another type of pilgrim, one who must be understood as he relates to the tale he tells. Not all of the tellers have specific relationships to their tales, but when such relationships do exist, they often support the interpretation of the pilgrimage and the game of tales which I am offering here. The Monk provides a simple example of the kind of pilgrim who markedly departs from what we know of his life's habits through the nature of the tale that he tells. In the General Prologue, he is presented satirically; he cares for nothing but temporal pleasures: hunting, eating, drinking, easy living—all the comforts which place a man at the mercy of Fortune. And yet, when he comes to his pilgrimage, he responds to the exhortation to "brek not oure game" by relating a series of *de casibus* tragedies:

> Tragedie is to seyn a certeyn storie
> As olde bookes maken us memorie,
> Of hym that stood in greet prosperitee,
> And is yfallen out of heigh degree
> Into myserie, and endeth wrecchedly.
> (7.1973–77)

He takes his subject matter from that realm of books and perpetual memory which, in Chaucer's scheme of thinking, is so importantly distinguished from temporal existence. And accordingly, the Monk's Tale stands in opposition to the spirit of his temporal life, a life in which the truth of tragedy is disregarded in riot and dissipation and in which books play no part:

> What sholde he studie and make hymselven wood,
> Upon a book in cloystre alwey to poure,
> Or swynken with his handes, and laboure,
> As Austyn bit? How shal the world be served?
> (1.184–87)

The world, in the Monk's Tale, is not served, for the conventional moral of tragedy in the Middle Ages is that men should turn their attention away from the world. The Monk is not a permanently changed man; we may expect him to return to "al his lust." Yet, for this occasion of pilgrimage and game, he has set aside his normal habits to think and "endite" on a different plane.

The Monk is not alone in lending this kind of structural principle to the *Canterbury Tales*. The Parson, though he occupies the opposite end of the moral spectrum, nevertheless functions similarly in Chaucer's fiction. His portrait is undoubtedly among the most complimentary in the Prologue, not least because of the active nature of his charity. While the Monk mocks toil, the Parson vigorously serves his parish daily, and part of his motive for doing so stems from his belief that men learn from good examples:

> This noble ensample to his sheep he yaf,
> That first he wroghte, and afterward taughte.
> (1.496–97)

> To drawen folk to hevene by fairness,
> By good ensample, this was his bisynesse.
> (1.519–20)

How is it possible for Chaucer to portray this model priest in such a way that he can significantly depart from his normal occupation without demeaning himself? The first answer is that the present pilgrimage offers a legitimate exception to one of the Parson's firmest rules:

> He sette nat his benefice to hyre
> And leet his sheep encombred in the myre
> And ran to Londoun unto Seinte Poules
> To seken hym a chaunterie for soules,
> Or with a bretherhed to been withholde;
> But dwelte at hoom, and kepte wel his folde,
> So that the wolf ne made it nat myscarie.
> (1.507–13)

Normally, the Parson remains in his parish as its spiritual protector, retiring neither for his own gain nor for seclusion. Yet he makes no apologies for leaving his sheep untended for the occasion of the Canterbury pilgrimage. Moreover, we can hardly doubt his intentions when we observe the importance of his sermon in ending the game of tales. Even there, however, departures from his normal procedure may be found. The Parson's portrait in the General Prologue stresses the fact that he acts first and preaches later, and that he teaches most effectively by example. But when the host asks him to tell his "greet metere" in the form of a fable, to tell an exemplary tale among the other stories, the Parson refuses and, instead, preaches a sermon. Appropriately, his decision seems to move the pilgrimage onto a higher level, and it does so because his *context* is essentially different from what it is in the parish. Here, he can point the way directly to "thilke parfit glorious pilgrymage / That highte Jerusalem celestial" precisely because he is participating in a pilgrimage in the first place. At home, his ambitions must be much humbler. In the ordinary world of travail and temptation, a priest does well to set a proper example for right action in mundane affairs; the way to salvation proceeds step by step through time. At the end of the Canterbury game, however, the pilgrims can "gladly heere" the Parson's comprehensive program for human salvation in its abstract entirety. The sermon has not lost its reference to life in this world, and the Parson remains recognizably himself; yet the perspective of his listeners has changed. They have been seeing the world, through fictions, from a distance, and their vision has acquired an unaccustomed scope. Thus, the Parson, like the other pilgrims, retains attributes which link him to his temporal life, but because some of those attributes do not apply in pilgrimage, he too demonstrates what kind of departure we and these pilgrims have made.

The question of perspective should affect our understanding of the Pardoner as well. His portrait records a life of extorting "offerings" and generally capitalizing on the needs and gullibilities of poor people. For success in this kind of deception, moreover, he needs one talent in particular:

> Wel koude he rede a lessoun or a storie.
> But alderbest he song an offertorie;
> For wel he wiste, when that song was songe,
> He moste preche and wel affile his tonge
> To wynne silver, as he ful wel koude.
>
> (1.709–13)

He must sing well and speak well, and the addresses which win him silver take the form of either a homiletic "lessoun" or a moral story. Thus, the Pardoner's Tale itself offers a superb example of its teller's "geere," the tool of his trade. His prologue, on the other hand, is a different matter. Before telling his tale, the Pardoner publicly denounces himself for his sin of avarice with the result that the tale itself, also an exposition of avarice, serves reflectively to condem the man who tells it. Now this procedure hardly represents the kind of rhetorical skills required by the Pardoner's vocation, and when, with his moral tale finished, he asks for money even from the host, Harry Bailly's response is a violent verbal attack. This ending often puzzles readers, but it can be understood in terms of a shift of perspective between the usual situation in which the Pardoner's tales are told and this occasion of pilgrimage. The Pardoner tells a brilliant moral tale, just as he customarily does to prepare listeners for his solicitations. This time, however, he has defeated any attempt to gull his companions by exposing his avarice before the tale is told. The spirit of penance and the resulting confessional candor which the pilgrimage engenders alter the perspective of the Pardoner's audience and thereby deprive his skill of its usual function. The Pardoner and most of the pilgrims seem to understand this perfectly well; Harry Bailly, on the other hand, does not. Swearing oaths like the rioters in the tale, he attacks the Pardoner ad hominem, mistakenly replacing game with an "earnest" reading of the invitation to worship the Pardoner's relics for a price.

The same disjunction between pilgrimage and ordinary life receives stress from several other sources, though in less complicated ways. The Wife of Bath comes to join the company, for example, at a time when she is not a wife. The Canon's Yeoman can defy and expose his master as he could never do under ordinary circumstances. And the clerk, man of few words and teacher of moral virtue, tells a tale whose moral issues are ultimately difficult to resolve and whose heroine is explicitly not recommended as a model for living wives. One of the most subtle exploitations of a pilgrim's movement out of his temporal life and values occurs in Chaucer's treatment of the Merchant. A shrewd bargainer, this "worthy man" does not hesitate to declare his mercenary system of values with the greatest conviction:

> His resons he spak ful solempnely,
> Sownynge alwey th'encrees of his wynnyng.
> (1.274–75)

But again we must look at the tale he tells. Paul A. Olson has shown that January, from the beginning, thinks of May in mercenary terms; she is treated as an object to be bought and possessed, with the result that January gives in to the jealousy which precipitates his cuckolding. Thus, in a tale which deals, like many others, with love and marriage, the Merchant's proudly espoused commercial values are shown—and by the Merchant himself—to be inappropriate to marriage, a kind of human "exchange" which clearly concerns him in a serious personal way.

Chauser did not "invent" the form of the *Canterbury Tales* (or the Prologue) ex nihilo. He had previously adapted an ancient convention, the rhetorical catalogue, to serve a new purpose in his early poems, the purpose of defining an extraordinary mode of human experience or knowledge. The alteration of function left the device of the catalogue with an immense new potential, one which Chaucer went on to explore by expanding it into the central organizing principle for his most ambitious poem. This, however, is only half an explanation. It locates a formal source and a continuity between the dream visions and the *Canterbury Tales*. But the latter is *not* a dream vision. Lacking a dream and a supernatural apparatus, it introduces a company of contemporary travelers and, most important, a competition as part of its fundamental structure. In asking why Chaucer chose the catalogue as an inchoate pattern on which to build, we must also ask why he built as he did, why the concerns of the earlier poems developed in this direction instead of some other. And here, since antecedents cannot entail their own transformations, we need to examine the relationship between literary change and a nonliterary social reality.

As I have said, the binary opposition between life in time and a timeless eternity becomes, in Chaucer's poetry, a triad. A third principle derives its elements from both of the prior categories in order to provide a tenuous and fleeting respite from temporal limitations without projecting the ultimate displacement of death itself. In the early poems the vehicles of transcendence are visionary and mythic, but, in the *Canterbury Tales,* Chaucer invents a human social institution with much the same implications. I think this literary evolution reflects a heightened anxiety about selective aspects of ordinary life in time, and we need to specify this anxiety in order to understand the literary change.

The Canterbury pilgrims come from various points of origin to share in cyclic, ritualized time through pilgrimage. Furthermore, they represent not only regions but a variety of different classes or social types. The interaction of these types provides the central dramatic principle of the journey, and, if I am correct, it also locates Chaucer's source of anxiety. In short, the relative accessibility of different social groups to one another was changing in fourteenth-century England, and the Canterbury pilgrimage posits an access which was, as yet, outside the realm of ordinary experience but which reflected some of the currents of contemporary change.

Social historians have shown that, during the fourteenth and fifteenth centuries, a system of social organization according to rank and fixed privilege gradually yielded to one based more nearly on our modern notion of class. In economic terms, this shift corresponds to various phases of the transition from the medieval feudal economy to a mercantile, proto-capitalist economy. Sylvia Thrupp, among others, has described both the growing centrality of competition in the restructured economy of the fourteenth century and the breakdown of regional economic insularity. As small communities increasingly took part in interregional trade, the influence of merchants in government grew, with consequences that affected the entire culture:

> Where this condition persisted for any length of time, social distinction hardened into the lines of a definite class structure, and political and economic crises were likely to generate class conflict.
>
> (*The Merchant Class of Medieval London*)

Social restructuring along class lines determined by wealth and economic function was not, of course, limited to provincial centers of craft and small trade. Persons of knightly rank, dependent on incomes from their lands or the meager proceeds of soldiering, often found themselves in the most serious kind of poverty, while wealthy merchants, lawyers, physicians, clerks and tradespeople, especially in London, were promoted to knightly rank, adopted heraldic arms or married their daughters into noble families. And the nobility in turn increasingly took up trade as a means of sustaining its status in fact as well as in name. These developments, which can only be glanced at here, brought with them new social freedoms and new dangers. There is, for example, substantial evidence to suggest that the late fourteenth and early fifteenth centuries allowed for new possibilities of intimacy and interpersonal exchange among persons of different professions or trades and among persons of different ranks. This is the constructive side. The destructive side is economic and class conflict.

Changes in social structure, of course, take time, and while they are in progress, they can be simultaneously frightening and fascinating to those who are involuntarily subject to their implications. Moreover, in periods of relatively rapid change, conservative customs and taboos tend to retain their strongest hold on individual behavior in the most familiar (and usually least urban) circumstances. I think, therefore, that we must see Chaucer's insistence on displacement from home, the introduction of pilgrimage as a special (though predictable) event, and the breadth of social representation among the pilgrims as formally related in a conceptual structure which reflects concrete social ambiguities and tensions. The pilgrimage is an occasion on which a kind of experimentation in social interaction is possible which is perhaps still less comfortable among peasants, craftsmen, monks, friars, pardoners, seamen, land holding widows, franklins, and nobles when all are part of the same small community. And this returns us to the question of anxiety.

If one consistent issue emerges from Chaucer's poetry, it is that of competition. Most obvious in the *Parlement of Foules, Troilus and Criseyde,* and the *Canterbury Tales,* it is nevertheless latent in the courtly love language of the *Book of the Duchess,* the dispensation of reputations in the *House of Fame,* and the implicitly comparative presentations of virtue in the *Legend of Good Women.* And in the stronger poems, the social grounding of the competitve anxiety emerges unambiguously: confusion about social rank or classes in the *Parlement,* the intrusion of war into interpersonal relations in the *Troilus,* and the alienating functions of economic relations in the *Canterbury Tales.* Conflict, class and money relate within the poems in varying proportions but will furnish, in nearly every case, the conditions of anxiety out of which Chaucer generates his alternative fictive spaces.

Thus, in a large number of cases, the details with which Chaucer chooses to locate his pilgrims in the actual world involve the ways they use or otherwise relate to money or wealth. The Monk is equivocal as a Monk not only because he loves the pleasure of hunting but because he possesses the fine horses, hounds, and gear to hunt in the grandest style. Of the Friar we know primarily his means of acquiring more income than he should. The Merchant is rich, the Clerk is poor, and both the Man of Law and the Franklin are distinguished chiefly by their abilities to expand their ownership of land, a function which, under a stricter feudal order would be confined to barons or other nobles. As money gains prestige, so do those whose living comes by wage or sale, and the guildsmen on the road to Canterbury are well aware that possessions are beginning to give them an unaccustomed status:

> For catel hadde they ynogh and rente,
> And eek hir wyves wolde it wel assente:
> And elles certeyn were they to blame.
> It is ful fair to been ycleped "madame,"
> And goon to vigilies al bifore,
> And have a mantel roialiche ybore.
> (1.373–78)

The Shipman is a petty thief, the Doctor of Physic loves gold above all else, and the figures of the Miller, Manciple, Reeve, Summoner, and Pardoner are all, to some degree, particularized and gently satirized according to their variously opportunistic participations in the economic order. Nevertheless, the designation of "good felawe" continues to recur, either in explicit terms of implicitly through the narrator's comradely affection. As companions in pilgrimage fellowship, Chaucer the pilgrim accepts them all, responding without reserve to those who exploit opportunities for economic advancement with the fewest scruples. Must we then conclude that our narrator lacks discrimination or is naive? To me, this question does not seem quite to the point. What I have been describing is a formal and ideational structure designed to separate pilgrimage from ordinary life on the grounds that economic or mercantile motives and practices lack their usual consequences in the context of fellowship as a ceremony of spring. In other words, Chaucer has invented formal devices, an expanded catalogue and a contest, which embrace social change at one level—the interaction among members of separate classes—while resisting the more ominous implications of that change at another level—the mutual human destructiveness inherent in economic competition.

This is not just a pilgrimage; it is a "game" played on a pilgrimage. And it is this fact which so compellingly diverts attention away from the ultimate "enjoyment" of the pilgrims' destination and toward the enjoyment of the journey for its own sake. St. Augustine would not have accepted the value of such diversion, but St. Augustine did not live in fourteenth-century England. Harry Bailly does. He has seen many pilgrims in his day, and he knows their needs well; he knows that those needs cannot be wholly fulfilled by worship at the shrine of a martyr:

> Ye goon to Caunterbury—God yow speede,
> The blisfil martir quite yow youre meed!
> And wel I woot, as ye goon by the weye,
> He shapen yow to talen and to pleye;
> For trewely, confort ne myrthe is noon
> To ride by the weye doumb as a stoon;
> And therfore wol I maken yow disport,
> As I seyde erst, and doon yow som confort.
> And if yow liketh alle by oon assent
> For to stonden at my juggement,
> And for to werken as I shal yow seye,
> To-morwe, whan ye riden by the weye,
> Now, by my fader soule that is deed
> But ye be myrie, I wol yeve yow myn heed!
> (1.769–82)

The host represents this need for "disport" or "pleye" as being no less fundamental than that of pilgrimage itself. And in order to confirm its particular function in the social context, we need only look to the specific formulation of the game.

The pilgrims will tell tales in a competition with a material commodity as prize, a dinner bought by the "losers." But, for those who pay, the loss is negligible; one dinner will be divided among twenty-nine purses. Indeed, there is only one way a pilgrim can incur financial hardship on this pilgrimage: to violate the rules of the game by depriving the host of his final judgment. In this case the offending pilgrim will pay "all that we spenden by the weye." Pilgrimage is, therefore, not merely an occasion of "escape" from ordinary life. It can incorporate the materially motivated competition on which the transformation of medieval society is based, but, at the level of consequences, it reduces that competition to a trivialized form. The members of different social groups can relate to one another in progressive ways derived from the flexible medium of monetary exchange; but none of them will be tempted to "enjoy" their new freedom by inflicting injury on others as they too often do in their actual lives. Nor will poverty or Christian charity be a handicap in Harry Bailly's game.

We have come a long way from the simple catalogue of trees in the

Parlement of Foules. Yet, in a sense, we have not come so far as it appears. Those trees, by making reference to the temporal reality of their uses, complicated the idea of a timeless garden; they made it a place which is neither this world nor eternity but something intermediate between them. The debate of the birds verified this implication by compromising between the discord of temporal conflict and the perfect harmony of the heavenly music. In a similar way the Canterbury pilgrims bring their temporal attributes into a ceremony which prefigures the celestial pilgrimage but which also reevaluates the daily lives of its participants. In both cases, Chaucer remains a poet who, in the words of J. A. W. Bennett, "hovers between two worlds, celestial and terrestrial" (*Chaucer's Book of Fame*).

As a final exercise, it should be possible to see why an ambivalence toward social transformations might manifest itself poetically in the refusal to accept time and timelessness as exclusive contexts for human life. The linear time of historical change suggests that no social institution is permanent, while the hierarchic structure of feudal society claims, through its analogical relation to the structure of the church, an eternal dispensation. To challenge either one of these conflicting orders in the terms provided by the other would not, for Chaucer, have been a possibility; the one was too immediate to experience, while the other was still to powerfully authoritative. What he could do was to accept the antithesis and to resolve it dialectically rather than preferentially. He is not, in this sense, displaying either conservatism or liberalism in his poetic statement. He creates an institution in which both the changeless and the changing take on new significance in relation to one another through the twin perspective of cyclic time and the possibilities of game in an unfamiliar social context. The dialectic itself and the *need* for resolution had been stated in the early dream visions. There, however, a problem born of social conflict could be solved only in terms of private experience. The final step to be taken was to return the poet's vision to concrete history, to seek a form of resolution in the human community itself. Chaucer was gesturing in this direction in the *Parlement* where "commun profit" is the central issue. But the filling out of the full social structure of exchange required a new poetic structure. Chaucer built that new form not out of the earlier genre but out of the convention within that genre which he had used to bring supernatural experience nearest to concrete reality. And that convention, in all its deceiving simplicity, was the rhetorical catalogue of types.

Creation in Genesis and Nature in Chaucer's General Prologue 1–18

Jane Chance

Literary antecedents of the opening lines of the Prologue to the *Canterbury Tales* include works of classical, medieval Latin, and Italian literature, and, more generally, the vernacular European lyric and the dream vision. But no scholar has yet fully realized, except in a general way, the specific thematic and structural indebtedness of these lines to the hexameral creation of the cosmos and its inhabitants in the book of Genesis—granted the caveat that no one source seems prototypical of the passage. This interest in the creation gained artistic currency as an ordering principle when it was used in the twelfth century to structure the Chartrian *Cosmographia* of Bernard Silvester, a work divided into two books to describe in the first the creation of the macrocosm and in the second that of the microcosm man. However, whereas Bernard employed the mythic figures of Noys [intelligence] and Endelechia [World Soul] to accomplish the initial creation of the Chain of Being in book 1, *Megacosmus*, and of Natura, Physis, and Urania to accomplish the initial creation of its crown, Man, in book 2, *Microcosmus*, Chaucer returns to a less fabulous and more biblical framework for the Prologue. Ending with the Revelation-like allusion to the Holy Jerusalem in the Parson's Prologue (followed appropriately by Chaucer's "Retraction," as if in fear of the Last Judgment), he begins equally appropriately with a Genesis-like opening.

The general correspondence between these first eighteen lines and the Hexameron and Fall is supported both by the time and purpose of the

From *Papers on Language and Literature* 14, no. 4 (Fall 1978).

pilgrimage and by the sequence of ideas and images ordering these lines. The first day of the world, according to Aelfric's translation of *De Temporibus Anni*, occurred on March 15, and the date of the pilgrimage, according to the reference to the sun's course through the Ram, occurs after April 11, time enough after the Fall. Secondly, as Ralph Baldwin has indicated, the reason for the pilgrimage derives from the Fall: like our first parents compelled to leave Eden we journey as on a pilgrimage through life to the Celestial City and Day of Judgment. But most importantly, the sequence of ideas and images in the *reverdie* is dictated by that of the Hexameron and Fall in Genesis.

Because the Fall has already taken place, Chaucer describes the recreation of the fallen world through Nature's various agents: she represents God's vicar. His concept of Nature drawn from Alain de Lille's in the twelfth-century *De Planctu Naturae* and expressed in the *Parlement of Foules* chiefly depends on two principles, *natura naturata* (the Nature that has been natured, or created originally, by God—the informed universe) and *natura naturans* (the Nature that continues to "nature" itself through perpetual renewal—the *procreatrix* as a secondary creative force in the universe). The created universe, as Alain's well-dressed goddess revealed, begins with the zodiacal crown of the heavens and ends with the flowers adorning her shoes, all mirroring, in effect, the Chain of Being. So Chaucer's Nature as an incarnation of order and hierarchy ("Nature, the vicaire of the almyghty Lord,/That hot,cold, hevy, lyght, moyst, and dreye/Hath knyt by evene noumbres of acord," [*Parlement of Foules* ll. 379–81]) presides over the congress of the four orders of fowl that represent the hierarchy of the four estates. In addition, as an incarnation of the principle of plenitude ("hot, cold, hevy, lyght, moyst, and dreye"), Nature invites all the species of birds to the meeting until the "erthe, and eyr, and tre, and every lake/So ful was, that unethe was there space/For me to stonde" (ll. 313–15). In the General Prologue, similarly, the description of *natura naturata* follows the hexameral sequence of the first chapter of Genesis in lines 1–11, culminating in lines 12–18 in a brief description of that epitome of Nature, Man. Both sections thus reflect the structural division of the *Cosmographia* of Bernard (subtitled *Megacosmus et Microcosmus*). The process of *natura naturans* in the Prologue appears in the power of wind and sun to prepare the world for new growth, in the drive of all creatures to reproduce, here denoted by the birds as a synedoche, and symbolically, supernaturally, in the impulse of man to renew himself spiritually through pilgrimage.

The Creation of the universe began when God first distinguished light from dark, or Day from Night, on the first day. So Nature's first action in the *reverdie* distinguishes the season of light, spring, from that of dark, winter. April has succeeded March ("Whan that Aprill with his shoures soote/The droghte of March hath perced to the roote," [ll. 1–2; F. N. Robinson, 2d ed.]), as the second half of Aries succeeds the first (ll. 7–8), as night succeeds day. The emphasis in both Genesis and the *reverdie* falls upon time limited and finite.

On the second day God shaped creation spatially, as he had done temporally on the first day, by separating the chaotic waters above from the waters below and thus creating the firmament of Heaven. As a result of this separation, commerce between the natural world and the supernatural one occurs primarily through the agents Providence, Fate, and Fortune. But note that Chaucer shows communication occurring not between the firmament and earth but between the lower aerial region below the moon and the earth: heavenly waters ("shoures soote") descend to earth (an act described as "piercing" or "bathing") where they "engender" the moisture of the sap vessels ("And bathed every veyne in swich licour"). The waters above join the waters below in an inverse act of creation.

On the third day of Creation dry lands separate from the seas and God produces plant life—grass, herbs, trees. Chaucer accordingly speaks of roots, sap vessels, the blooming flower, "tendre croppes" (ll. 2, 3, 4, 6, 7). On the fourth day He fashions the luminaries of the sun, moon, and stars; similarly Chaucer remarks on the position of the "yonge sonne" who "Hath in the Ram his halve cours yronne" (l. 8). Further, the description of the "smale foweles" making melody throughout the night (l. 9) acts as a synecdoche for the fowl of the air created on the fifth day, followed by the allusion to folk and palmers seeking pilgrimage (ll. 12–13), itself a synecdoche for the creation of mankind on the sixth day.

The consequences of the Fall following the six days of Creation find expression in the first eighteen lines through the emphasis on change and mutability affecting both Nature the macrocosm and human nature the microcosm. The "sickness" of the world (winter, drought, dryness) is "healed" in the spring; similarly the spiritual sickness of the "little world" is healed in part by pilgrimage to the shrine of St. Thomas à Becket. But even physically ill in the past, they now march to Canterbury "The hooly blisful martir for to *seke*, /That hem hath holpen whan that they were *seeke*" (ll. 17–18, my italics). Memory of man's infirmities as exemplifications of postlapsarian mutability impels the quest in gratitude, in seeking: Chaucer uses homonyms, i.e., identical rhyme, to draw attention to the causal relationship between "sickness" and "seeking" and thereby remind the reader of the need of man, pricked within his *corage* by memory, to act as his own recreator.

This hexameral classification of Nature into a hierarchy in the first part of the *reverdie* (ll. 1–11) parallels the similar but brief catalogue of human nature in the second part (ll. 12–18). The microcosm reflects the macrocosm in terms of a human chain of being that conveys the principles of order and plenitude witnessed in the natural Chain of Being. The most ordinary human type consists of "folk" aspiring to be pilgrims; there exist as well professional pilgrims, or palmers. Chaucer amplifies his distinction by a curious antithesis: the professional pilgrims seek shrines in strange lands, moving from a fixed point outward, centripetally, toward many loci. However, the Canterbury pilgrims drawn "from every shires ende" (l. 15), or from many places, move centrifugally inward toward a fixed point, the shrine of St. Thomas. In addition, the two motives, to travel as an end in itself and to travel as a means to the end of penance, underscored by this difference in motions, neatly differentiate worldly pleasure from a more otherworldly form, and as well two types of human nature. These two Chaucer contrasts with a third, the "hooly blisful martir" St. Thomas (l. 17), a truly perfect saintly human being. (Perhaps the catalogue actually ends with the Parson's allusion to Christ at the very end of the *Tales*.) This "human chain of being" is analogous to the natural Chain of Being presented in the first eleven lines and elaborates the orderly social classification of human beings in the General Prologue and the *Tales* themselves.

As Nature also consists of renewing itself, of the process of "naturing" nature to maintain the Chain of Being, her agents of rain, wind, and sun in this passage echo the original Creation of the universe by God. First, like a natural Father, April re-creates through reproductive metaphors joining heaven and earth—sexually piercing or penetrating the roots below ground, bathing the sap vessels with sufficient moisture to "engender" the flower (ll. 1–4). Then Zephirus—a pagan Holy Ghost—"with his sweete breeth / Inspired hath in every holt and heeth / The tendre croppes" (ll. 5–7). The mythic and classical third person of the Trinity (here God's vicar Nature) uses the balmy winds from the heavens to inspire or breathe into the tender twigs of the woodlands and the heath above ground. Finally, the pun on sun and son ("yonge sonne") alerts the reader to the analogy between the second person of the Trinity and the astrological Son who, far above ground, passes through the first sign of the Zodiac to remind man of the time of the original Creation of the world and of the reason for his later need to redeem man through his own Incarnation in flesh.

The naturing of cosmic Nature finds a spiritual equivalent in human nature. The pilgrim represents the human equivalent of April, Zephirus, and the sun as pilgrimage represents an analogue to the motion of showers descending, the west wind blowing, the sun entering a new sign. In the space of eighteen lines Chaucer thus reflects the difficulties of man in understanding and coping with the regeneration of his nature in a postlapsarian world continually regenerating itself in opposition to chaos, death, nothingness—a proper prolegomenon to the specific examples provided in the General Prologue and the tales themselves.

Gold and Iron: Semantic Change and Social Change in Chaucer's Prologue

Geoffrey Hughes

In the proem to the second book of *Troilus & Criseyde*—"litel min tragedie," as Chaucer was to call it with considerable semantic licence—we find these famous lines:

> Ye knowe ek that in forme of speche is chaunge
> Withinne a thousand yeer, and wordes tho
> That hadden pris, now wonder nyce and straunge
> Us thinketh hem; and yit they spake hem so,
> And spedde as wel in love as men now do:
> Ek for to winnen love in sondry ages,
> In sondry londes sondry ben usages.

These observations on linguistic change in general and semantic change in particular do not now appear to be very remarkable, until one tries to parallel them. They are uttered in a deceptively self-effacing manner, as if the narrator does not want to bore anyone by expatiating on obviosities well within the range of any observant person's awareness. Today the evidence of semantic change is all around us: the scholar observes a great deal of it with feelings of quiet desperation. The invention of moveable type has stabilized the form but has been used, as some would say, to "destabilize the semantic content" of language. Chaucer's prayer, at the end of his great work that it be faithfully reproduced amidst the "gret diversité in Englissh" has eventually been answered, but with a vengeance.

Today Chaucer's lines have an added irony, which one can be sure,

From *Standpunte 137* 31, no. 5 (October 1978).

he would have relished, in that his *sentence* has been conclusively demonstrated by the striking semantic changes undergone in the last six hundred years by the very words he has chosen: words such as *pris, nyce* and *spedde,* to take only the most obvious examples. Furthermore, there is in these lines an explicit emphasis on change of register, on "wordes that hadden *pris*" (value or class or quality) having become "wonder nyce and straunge." Chaucer, as might be expected of a master of medieval rhetoric, has seen this basic separation of registers, which is largely a legacy of the Norman Conquest, and he exploits it in two basic ways: in the words with which he clothes and limits his characters; and the language with which he makes them clothe and limit their narratives. It is to his first variety of linguistic fashion that I should now like to turn, considering three basic examples, before relating Chaucer's manipulation of language to the social developments of his time.

The identification of character and word within the Prologue is quite as strong as that between character and *habit* or *custom* in their medieval senses of "clothes." Indeed the natural mode of discussing the Prologue is a kind of paraphrase larded with quotations, since they provide the indispensable *mots justes* combining outward description and authorial insight. And within the multiplex subtlety of mode and tone there is a quite deliberate, though more concealed exploitation of register and what one might call the "vintage" of language, to chose a metaphor which suits with Chaucer's origins. The Miller, for instance, is created—not simply defined—in all his dense physicality in old, rude, unpolished, powerfully monosyllabic words—Saxon and Norse—"words as deep as England," possessing a rock-like solidity:

> The Millere was a stout carl for the nones,
> Ful big he was of brawn and eek of bones;
> That proved wel, for overal ther he cam,
> At wrastling he wolde have alwey the ram.
> He was short-sholdred, brood, a thicke knarre;
> Ther was no dore that he nolde heve of harre,
> Or breke it at a renning with his heed.

Even the French borrowings, *stout* and *brawn,* lose any associations of refinement that they might once have had when placed in such knotted and gnarled native company. One could hardly imagine—but Chaucer did—a more extraordinary contrast than this:

> And sikerly she was of greet disport,
> And ful plesaunt and amable of port,

And pened hir to countrefete cheere
Of court, and to been estatliche of manere,
And to ben holden digne of reverence.

Madame Eglentine (as she would, no doubt, insist upon being called) is as ridiculously over-refined as the Miller is comically coarse, and so Chaucer has created her entirely in the language of effete, frenchified cliché, an idiom which is starting to sound rather jaded around 1386 when French, no longer the language of power, is rapidly going out of fashion, and Norman French would be something of a joke dialect, as Cornish would be today. Without knowing it, the Prioress shows the worst failing known to those who aspire to be fashionable: she is out of date.

Set against these two portraits, that of the worthy Knight gains an added verbal and moral significance, since it is a balanced blend of Saxon solidity and French subtlety, of

Trouthe and honoure, fredom and curteisne.

The Knight combines the best of the old and the new, lion in battle, lamb in hall, gallant but not gallánt. Yet almost every major word has changed semantically by becoming moralized (like *gentle*), or democatized (like *freedom* and *curteisie*).

Chaucer's perception that language is both "common," i.e., traditional and general, as well as individual becomes the great creative achievement in the artistry of the *Canterbury Tales*. By developing this insight he is able to explore the subtle modulation between teller and tale which makes him a genius incomparably greater, I rashly suggest, than Boccaccio, whose "originality" is so often given undue prominence. The comic diversity of language and insight first dramatised in the *Parlement of Foules* gives way to the tragic diversity of *Troilus & Criseyde* where Troilus is limited in language and thought by courtly convention, while Criseyde takes on, as Muscatine observed, the character and outlook of both Troilus's idealism and Pandarus's pragmatism; and the Pandar himself, the "doer the fixer," exists entirely in the pale of words. His role comes to an end, appropriately, when he says

I can no more seye!

In the broad texture of the Tales the anxieties, values and ambitions of the tellers are revealed by means of an authorial insight worthy of Freud, but more complex. The more obvious of these psychological revelations include the Pardoner's tale of darkness, disease, betrayal and death; the Wife of

Bath's wish-fulfilled returned to youthful sexual attractiveness, and the Franklin's anxiety about his own status as he watches artisans rising in wealth and importance all around him, an anxiety which is shown in the excessive quality of his *largesse,* the excessive quantity of rhetoric in his tale, and its obsession with *gentilesse* and *fredom,* which he presents in essentially competitive terms. His uncouth interruption of the Squire's Tale earns him a just rebuke from the Host, but only after he has revealingly praised this "rhetorically inept" performance, as Stanley Kahrl has described it (in "Chaucer's Squire Tale and the Decline of Chivalry," *Chaucer Review* 7 [1972]: 194–209). Furthermore, the Franklin shows unambiguously his confusion of noble values and the price of land, as if one can be used to obtain the other.

The tales of the trio of characters previously discussed are projections of their personalities in which the semantic content is an indispensably revealing factor. The grave formality of the Knight's Tale and its essentially high style are the suitable mode for a movingly noble effort to contain man's martial and erotic impulses as they develop out of a love triangle. The tragic or pathetic awareness that the outcome cannot be satisfactory for all is sublimiated by low-register asides and proverbial remarks. A whole range of register is thus used, just as there is a whole range of perspective from "The Firste Moevere" to the two dogs fighting over a bone. The goliardic parody of the Miller's Tale is obvious in its broad action and theme: the restrictions of convention, even the walls of the Knight's Tale, of Emily's garden, of the prisoners' dungeon, of the gods' temples are easily demolished by a narrator who, after all, likes knocking down doors with his skull; the action, which reflects the narrow physicality of the Miller's worldview is also, as John Leyerle has pointed out, very concerned with holes. The exactness of the language parody is inseparable from the action: the "noble duk" Theseus is replaced a "riche gnof" and a poignant line from the doomed Arcite's death speech:

Allone, withouten any compaignie

is exactly repeated, but with *compaignie* now carrying a strong sexual innuendo which is extended to *solas, pleye, instrument* and *pryvetee*. The low-register words, though apparently "common," are, in fact, frequently nonce words or unique in Chaucer's work. They are not simple "cherles termes," they are the Miller's words and include, as E. Talbot Donaldson has shown: *gnof, popelote, prymerole, piggesnye, lendes* and *squaymous*. The Prioress (the singing nun) manages to combine sentimentality and insensitivity in her tale of the singing martyr. She further sets the stamp of her personality on it, making it "semely" to God through nasalized forms, stilted inversions, aureate diction, references to expensive jewelry, and plenty of schmaltz.

II

As was observed earlier, the Franklin's wishful tale is concerned with what C. S. Lewis has termed the "moralisation" of *fredom*, a semantic change which has been taking place in the word in the course of the fourteenth century. The word, together with its relations *frank* and *liberal*, moves from being a denotative term of status in a static social system to become a more evaluative term allowing for individual merit and social mobility. Though his tale ends with a question: "Which was the mooste fre, as thinketh yow?" he clearly wished his audience to accept that *fredom* has undergone semantic change, that the quality is no longer transmitted by exclusive genetic privilege, and that through his wealth the Franklin will be able to make an entry into the pages of Burke's *Peerage*. His favourite bedside reading, we may suppose, would be conservative interpretations of the Peasants' Revolt, such as the *Anonimalle Chronicle*. This describes how the merchants William Wälworth, Nicholas Bramber, Robert Launde and John Philpot were duly knighted for services rendered in the suppression of the Peasants' Revolt, and by way of a gold pot at the end of the rainbow,

> the king gave Sir William Walworth 100 pounds in land,
> and each of the others 40 pounds in land, for them and their
> heirs.

But, as Morton Bloomfield's "querulous objector" would interpose, isn't all this a bit fanciful? We don't know, and perhaps care less, what the Franklin read. Chaucer, after all, mentions the Peasants' Revolt on en passant, via the Nun's Priest, and even there he seems to be making a point more about crowd psychology than politics, of how the chase after Chantecleer and the colfox takes on, consecutively, elements of a carnival, a riot, and apocalyptic chaos, before the object is forgotten about altogether. It seems to be a remark on the ironic nature of popular movements. It takes an imaginative (and undisciplined) foreigner like Froissart to assert economic and social causes for the revolt with complete confidence as when he develops the old religious saw

> Whanne Adam dalfe and Eve span
> Who was thanne a gentil man?

into a most moving appeal for social equality. And, given the wide semantic parameters of common words in Middle English, cannot a whole range of resonances be inferred or attributed to them? Further, D. W. Robertson, Jr., has taken the view that "the medieval world was innocent of our profound concern for tension." He insists that "We project dynamic polarities on history as class struggles, balances of power, or as conflicts between economic realities and traditional ideals" and that "the medieval world with its quiet hierarchies knew nothing of these things."

Robertson's arguments are weighty and far-reaching in their implications. Projection, it must be conceded, is a noted intellectual disease, not least since it derives from one of the ways in which we "make sense" as we put it, of the world. Is history made by assertive minorities or silent majorities? And, even when one has arrived at some intelligently flexible notion of history, is literature's symbiosis with history based on compensation or imitation? How do we know when a writer is using rose-tinted spectacles, dark glasses or blinkers?

A serious objection is that *Preface to Chaucer* contains no references in its 500-plus pages to the Peasants' Revolt, Wat Tyler or John Ball, that grey eminence. References to the Black Death are purely aesthetic, suggesting it as a cause for the stylistic break (in stone carving) between the first and second halves of the fourteenth century, and connecting it with the emergence of realism. This bland aesthetic treatment of the most violent upheavals of fourteenth-century England suggests that perhaps the notion of "quiet hierarchies" is a projection itself, one sustained not so much by absence as by suppression of evidence.

For, even if one rejects all the chronicles, not just those which are clearly biased, such as that of Walsingham, or contain marginal deficiencies, such as that of Knighton, there is still a great deal of suggestive legal evidence showing the growth of an acquisitive, competitive, profit-oriented ethos occasioned by the labour shortages caused in turn by the Black Death. The Statute of Labourers (1351) which tried to keep wages down; the abortive Sumptuary Ordinance (1363) which, comically, tried to keep appearances down; the Poll Tax which tried to keep the disastrous foreign war going; the Charters of Manumission (granted to the peasants at the height of the revolt) and their revocation; the Acts against the Lollards, all of these show the "quiet hierarchies" in obvious turmoil within themselves and in conflict with each other. It is precisely out of this turmoil that Chaucer shows character and values being formed, and terms of value being distorted by semantic changes contingent upon those social changes.

III

The central notion which is changing is that of *profit*. The old formula *commune profit* (found in the Clerk's Tale) gives way to private profit, as *common weal* gave way to *private wealth,* and in each case the profiteering is achieved by violent competition, casual preemption of established privilege and cynical exploitation of the poor or underprivileged. It is significant, therefore, that the two major feuds of the pilgrimage, between Miller and Reeve, and Summoner and Friar, can be interpreted as having their origins in economic competition. The Summoner is swift to discredit a rival:

> Lo, goode men, a flye and eek a frere
> Wol falle in every dyssh and eek mateere.

They are both of them "flyes" and the "dyssh" is the lucrative market of confession which they and the pardoner are "bisily" converting into a riot of "pay as you sin." It is inadequate to assert, as Robertson does, that the Miller "is the very picture of *discordia,*" since this imposes an undue limitation on both the Miller and *discordia*. Discordia must have a large family, almost by definition. And though, as I believe, Chaucer is showing Miller and Reeve as traditional enemies tied together in endless seasonal friction by the cash nexus, he is no doctrinaire Marxist, since first, they should be on the same side of the class struggle, and second, he created them as two wily, professional thieves, and worse (for them) as physical and mental "antitypes": the brutal extrovert who likes a good, vinous dirty joke; and the mean misanthrope, who keeps well away from the *compaignie*.

This suggests, negatively, that Chaucer believes as much in "force of character" as he does in "social forces." The positive endorsement of his faith lies in his creation on those idealised representative of the Three Estates who still regard social life as, literally, the "life of friends" and fraternity as a social ideal rather than an economic grouping. The upheavals of the past years have left no ferment in them. They do not, accordingly, take the opportunity of telling a tale to grind some private axe, as the Man of Law does in his story of the dutifully submissive Constance, which, however, Sheila Delany has seen as *Chaucer's* "reaffirmation of the hierarchical values which had so recently and so sharply been attacked." One might as well apply Gloucester's philosophy in *King Lear* to Shakespeare. A comic and ironic manifestation of forceful personality lies in the Wife of Bath's rejection of traditional "hierarchical values" and her assertion in their stead of a subversive regiment of women. In her studied inversion of traditional feudal order women achieve, not just liberation but *maistrie* (a term she does *not* feminize) and men have to offer *land, tresor* and *swinke,* which by an ingenious refinement of parody she interprets as a sexual "obligation of labour" or *sevitium debitum.* (Miller, Reeve and Host make the same sexual extension of meaning.) But the Man of Law has had, semantically speaking, the last word. Taking the solid grounds of misogyny and adding some xenophobia of the anti-Muslim variety, he brings out all his heavy legal rhetoric to denounce the devious sultaness of his tale:

> O sowdanesse, roote of iniquitee!
> Virgo thou, Semyrame the secounde,
> O serpent, under femynynytee,
> Lik to the serpent depe in helle ybound!

Unwittingly, but not surprisingly, he has launched a new term of sexual abuse: *virago,* to join *termagant, scold* and *shrew.*

Revolutionaries with powerful personalities and flamboyant lifestyles are seldom successful since they outrage the conservative and alienate the majority of the undecided but potentially sympathetic. Hence the Wife of Bath has been consigned into the realm of the Amazonian caricature, whence she is resuscitated as a historical curiosity. A more subtle eroder of established hierarchy and a more subtle exploiter of semantic licence is the Frair, who has enough "charismatic" versatility to be a "limitour," a confessor, a singer of "yeddinges," a "champioun," a go-between on "love-dayes," as well as a dubious marriage-broker. He seeks to discredit the whole of the ecclesiastical hierarchy by pretending to sympathize with the "pecunyal peyne" felt by the "smale tythers," cunningly implying that the tithe is a means of cruel exploitation, whereas the pitaunce of alms, because freely given, is not. His hypocrisy, his monstrous parody of Franciscan gentleness, serves to intensify his alienation from human sympathy, for he values people, not as individuals, but as commodities of different market worth. He thus has a hatred of the *poraille*—because of his exploitation of them—and an ingratiating servility towards the *riche:*

> And over al theras profit sholde arise
> Curteis he was and lowely of service
> Ther nas no man nowher so vertuous.

His abuse of his office is as studied as Chaucer's ironic misapplication of *curteis, lowely of service* and *vertuous.* In the last of these a pre-echo of *virtuosity* can, perhaps, be distantly heard: the irony seems to be more than a simple one. Confession is for him, after all, not a crude fleecing affair, but a delicate fusion of business with pleasure in which the languages of love and religion are delicately interwoven:

> Full swetely herde he confessioun,
> And pleasaunt was his absolucioun.
> He was an esy man to yeve penaunce
> Theras he wiste to have a good pitaunce.

Semantic interlace is thus used by Chaucer to show the ultimate simoniac corruption of the charming Friar. The "sacramental" words become tainted through "daliaunce and fair langage" on the one hand, and the terms of "profit" on the other, for example, *cost, ferme, purchas* and *rente*. Some of these sacramental words, such as *pitaunce,* preserve a suggestion of their religious origins. Others, such as *solempne,* have become almost entirely secularized. Chaucer deploys the word with systematic, though unobstrusive, irony of the Guildsmen, the Friar and the Merchant, all of them highly acquisitive people who have become obsessed with their own importance. Only the Parson uses the word in its older, religious sense: "The speces of Penitence been three. That oon of hem is solempne, another is commune, and the thridde is privee." *Reverence* is used in a similarly ironic manner to reveal the confused materialism of the Prioress, the pomposity of the speculating Sergeant, and the rather distant social manner of the Clerk. *Reverence* is, specifically, *not* one of the aims of the Parson, who is simply "a good man," just as his brother is a "trewe swinkere," an equally unusual, indeed unique, occurrence in the Prologue. The Knight is, likewise, the only unambiuously "worthy man."

IV

As was mentioned in the discussion of the Franklin's *fredom* and *gentilesse,* the upwardly mobile are knocking on the gates of the nobility or buying their way in. It is a time, therefore, of imitations. For instance, the Knight's disciplined, hierarchical service in "his lordes werre" is an essential part of his *chivalrye*; his son's *chivachye* is characteristically the less ordered, more flamboyant cavalry expedition, such as that of John of Gaunt from Calais to Bordeaux: magnificent but useless, in fact, possibly disastrous. The Merchant's *chevissaunce* takes the horse out of chivalry, etymologically speaking, and turns it into *usury*. This undisciplined, competitive acquisitiveness becomes virtually the opposite quality, but has a deceptive, pseudoaristocratic appearance, just as the Merchant does himself:

> So estatly was he of his governaunce.

Though apparently in debt, he is very fashionably dressed up for the pilgrimage. He speaks with the assured pomposity of a proto-capitalist,

> Sowinge alwey the'encrees of encrees of his *winning*.

He makes money of the currency blackmarket, thereby usurping the royal prerogative on foreign exchange dealings; but he depends parasitically on the king's authority to keep the sea clear of pirates. Not for the first time is the foreign beaver hat dependent on the rusty mail coat.

The different nuances surrounding words of acquisition such as *winning* form one of the most interesting semantic threads of the Prologue. The Knight has been at "Alisaundre . . . whan it was wonne," and his selfless, martial service has been largely for *cristendom* in all corners of the known world. The Merchant's entirely selfish mode of *winning* makes him obsessed with the one waterway which affects his corner of the market:

> He wolde the see were kepte for anything
> Bitwixe Middelburh and Orewelle.

The Doctor not only profits from disaster in that

> He kepte that he *wan* in pesitlence

but he also has a rapaciously efficient arrangement with "hise apothecaries" whereby

> . . . ech of hem made other for to *winne*.

And our final image of the Pardoner is of him "tuning-up" with a loud and merry Offertory before using his preaching

> To *winne* silver as he ful wel coude.

He has a narcissistic pride in his "turn":

> Myne handes and my tonge goon so yerne
> That it is joye to se my *bisynesse*.

The Parson, who does not see the world as a stage, leads a life devoted to the word's notion of virtuous diligence:

> To drawen folk to hevene by fairnesse
> By good ensample, this was his *bisynesse*.

And between the two, between the outrageously cynical profit-motivation of the Pardoner and the religious dedication of the Parson is the Clerk, praying *bisily* for the souls of his importuned sponsors.

Bisynesse thus stands—together with *profit* and *winne*—at an ethical and semantic crossroads. They can pass down the way of true fellowship, of harmonious *caritas*; or down that of false fellowship, or alienating, competitive *cupiditas*. (One comes back, predictably, to the same simple themes, the same threads which Ruth Nevo and Arthur Hoffman have explicated in this rich and subtle work.) For Chaucer created in the ideally charitable and "profitable" representatives of the Three Estates essentially simple, limited "goode men" who appear, ironically, rather uninteresting figures, without "character" or "personality." He observed in the corrupt and fallen ecclesiastics an alienation bred of materialism which is destructive spiritually, psychologically and socially. He showed the "gold" of the clergy rusting into interestingly unnatural shapes as its currency became debased, and the "iren" of the Third Estate becoming eroded as it became gilded. The humanity of the secular figures, even the extraordinary, triumphant vitality of the Wife of Bath, is limited by competitive materialism. Those "bran-new people" the Guildsmen, the Veneerings of the fourteenth century, who achieve material "success" are so boringly predictable in their aspirations that they can be given a corporate identity. They are a faceless set, cluttered with shining new "gere" and traditional old words. But the New Man of the meritocracy is the Maunciple (though one can see New Men appearing at all stages, just as the middle classes seem always to be rising). For he is the most successful profiteer or "winner" of all, and he is—uniquely—without personality, character or even body. He has no frame, no array, no mask. He is pure native wit, honed by the hardness of the market place. *He* does not need the security, let alone the uniform, of a "solempne and a greet fraternitee." He is the perfect, smooth administrator who can achieve anything, and feel nothing, the Machiavellian proptotype. One word gives us a clue to his sinister origins. In the second line we are told that "achatours might take example" from him. In Statute 36 of Edward III (1360) it is enacted "Que le heignous noun de *pourveyor* soit chaungé & nomé achatour." The purveyors had become so unpopular that their name was changed by the cynical substitution of terms to which we now give the name of "Orwellian." Not surprisingly, his tale is about the changing of *wyf* into *lemman* and *white* into *black*.

Chaucer shows in his deployment of nonce words, key words, status terms and moral terms, that character and language are inseparable, that words and values change as societies change, that the only true value attaches to virtue, which must be sought beyond the flux of words, since terms of value are particularly vulnerable to change in the hands of the ambitious. In the Prologue he prefers the mode of artistic irony; in his poem on *Gentilesse* he is explicit:

> For unto vertu longeth dignitee,
> And nought the revers, saufly dar I deeme,
> Al were mitre, crowne, or diademe.

The Art of Impersonation: A General Prologue to the *Canterbury Tales*

H. Marshall Leicester, Jr.

> *Nec illud minus attendendum esse arbitror, utrum . . . magis secundum aliorum opinionem quam secundum propriam dixerint sententiam, sicut in plerisque Ecclesiastes dissonas diversorum inducit sententias, imo ut tumultuator interpretatur, beato in quarto dialogorum attestante Gregorio.*
>
> *(In my judgment it is no less necessary to decide whether sayings found [in the sacred writings and the Fathers] are quotations from the opinions of others rather than the writers' own authoritative pronouncements. On many topics the author of Ecclesiastes brings in so many conflicting proverbs that we have to take him as impersonating the tumult of the mob, as Gregory points out in his fourth Dialogue.)*
>
> Peter Abelard

In his much praised book *The Idea of the* Canterbury Tales, Donald R. Howard has isolated a perennial strand in the Chaucer criticism of the last thirty years or more—isolated it, defined it clearly, and given it a name. Discussing the Knight's Tale, he remarks:

> Chaucer . . . introduced a jocular and exaggerated element that seems to call the Knight's convictions into question. For example, while the two heroes are fighting he says "in this wise I let hem fighting dwelle" and turns his attention to Theseus:
>
> The destinee, ministre general,
> That executeth in the world over all

From *PMLA* 95, no. 2 (March 1980).

The purveiaunce that God hath seen biforn,
So strong it is that, though the world had sworn
The contrary of a thing by ye or nay,
Yet sometime it shall fallen on a day
That falleth nat eft within a thousand yeer.
For certainly, our appetites here,
Be it of wer, or pees, or hate, or love,
All is this ruled by the sight above.
This mene I now by might Theseus,
That for to hunten is so desirous,
And namely at the grete hert in May,
That in his bed there daweth him no day
That he nis clad, and redy for to ride
With hunt and horn and houndes him beside.
For in his hunting hath he swich delit
That it is all his joy and appetit
To been himself the grete hertes bane.
For after Mars he serveth now Diane.

(ll. 1663–82)

All this machinery is intended to let us know that on a certain day Theseus took it in mind to go hunting. It is impossible not to see a mock-epic quality in such a passage, and hard not to conclude that its purpose is ironic, that it is meant to put us at a distance from the Knight's grandiose ideas of destiny and make us think about them. This humorous element in the Knight's Tale is the most controversial aspect of the tale: where one critic writes it off as an "antidote" to tragedy another puts it at the center of things, but no one denies it is there. It introduces a feature which we will experience in many a tale: we read the tale as a dramatic monologue spoken by its teller but understand that some of Chaucer's attitudes spill into it. This feature gives the tale an artistry which we cannot realistically attribute to the teller: I am going to call this *unimpersonated artistry*. In its simplest form it is the contingency that a tale not memorized but told impromptu is in verse. The artistry is the author's, though selected features of the pilgrim's dialect, argot, or manner may still be impersonated. In its more subtle uses it allows a gross or "low" character to use language, rhetoric, or wit above his capabilities. (Sometimes it is coupled with an impersonated *lack*

> of art, an artlessness or gaucherie which causes a character to tell a bad tale, as in *Sir Thopas,* or to violate literary conventions or proprieties, as in the Knight's Tale.) The effect is that of irony or parody, but this effect is Chaucer's accomplishment, not an impersonated skill for which the pilgrim who tells the tale deserves any compliments.

Having generated this principle, Howard goes on to apply it, at various points in the book, to the tales of the Miller, the Summoner, the Merchant, the Squire, and the Manciple. He is in good and numerous company. One thinks of Charles Muscatine's characterization of certain central monologues in *Troilus:* "the speeches must be taken as impersonal comments on the action, Chaucer's formulation, not his characters' "; of Robert M. Jordan, who, having presented an impressive array of evidence for a complicated Merchant in the Merchant's Tale, argues from it, like Dryden's Panther, "that he's not there at all"; of Anne Middleton's exemption of selected passages of the Physician's Tale from the pilgrim's voicing; of Robert B. Burlin's praise of the Summoner's Tale despite its being "beyond the genius of the Summoner"; and of many other commentators on the Knight's Tale, some of whom I mention later.

Now in my view this "unimpersonated artistry" is a problem, and a useful one. Howard's formulation—an attempt to describe an aspect of Chaucer's general practice—is valuable because it brings into the sharp relief of a critical and theoretical principle something that is more diffusely present in the practical criticism of a great many Chaucerians: the conviction, often unspoken, that at some point it becomes necessary to move beyond or away from the pilgrim narrators of the *Canterbury Tales* and to identify the poet himself as the source of meaning. If the assumption is stated this generally, I probably agree with it myself, but Howard's way of putting it does seem to me to reflect a tendency, common among Chaucer critics, to invoke the poet's authority much too quickly. Howard helps me to focus my own discontent, not with his criticism (much of which I admire), but with a more general situation in the profession at large. If we consider "unimpersonated aritstry" as a theoretical proposition, it seems open to question on both general and specific grounds; that is, it seems both to imply a rather peculiar set of assumptions to bring to the reading of any text and, at least to me, to be an inaccurate reflection of the experience of reading Chaucer in particular.

"Unimpersonated artistry" implies a technique, or perhaps an experience, of reading something like this: we assume that the Canterbury tales are, as they say, "fitted to their tellers," that they are potentially dramatic monologues or, to adopt what I hope is a less loaded term, that they are instances of *impersonated* artistry, the utterances of particular pilgrims. After all, we like to read Chaucer this way, to point out the suitability of the tales to their fictional tellers, and most of us, even Robert Jordan, would agree that at least some of the tales, and certainly the Canterbury frame, encourage this sort of interpretation. We read along, then, with this assumption in mind, until it seems to break down, until we come across a passage that we have difficulty reconciling with the sensibility—the temperament or the training or the intelligence—of the pilgrim in question. At that point, alas, I think we too often give up. "This passage," we say, "must be the work of Chaucer the poet, speaking over the head or from behind the mask of the Knight or the Miller or the Physician, creating ironies, setting us straight on doctrine, pointing us 'the righte weye.' " Unfortunately, these occasions are seldom as unequivocal as the one case of genuine broken impersonation I know of in the *Tales,* the general narrator's "quod she" in the middle of a stanza of the Prioress's Tale (7.1771; line numbers conform with F. N. Robinson, 2d ed.). Different critics find the poet in different passages of the same tale and often have great difficulty in deciphering his message once they *have* found him—a difficulty that seems odd if Chaucer thought the message worth a disruption of the fiction.

Thus, Howard, whose observations on the critical disagreement over the humorous element in the Knight's Tale are well taken, offers an interpretation of "The destinee, ministre general" that is in fact uncommon. His account of the ironic tone of these lines in context is at least more attentive to the effect of the language than are the numerous readings that take the passage relatively straight. Even within this group, however, the range of proposed answers to the question "Who's talking here?" is sufficiently various to raise the issue I am interested in. To mention only those who discuss this particular passage, Frost, Ruggiers, and Kean are representative of the large body of criticism that remains relatively inattentive to the whole question of voicing in the tale. They share a view of the passage as a piece of "the poem's" doctrine, to be taken seriously as part of an argument about man's place in the cosmos. Of those who, like Howard, find something odd about the passage, Burlin suggests that the speaker is Chaucer, who intends to suggest by it that Theseus is a man superior to Fortune but unaware of Providence, while Neuse, the only critic to attribute the speech unequivocally to the Knight, maintains that it differentiates the latter's implicitly Christian view of the story from Theseus's more limited vision. Who *is* talking here, and to what end? One might ask what the consequences for interpretation are if one concedes both that the passage makes gentle fun of the machinery of destiny, at least as applied to so trivial an event, and that it is the Knight himself who is interested in obtaining this effect. Howard's suggestion to the contrary, the passage is not really directed at Theseus's hunting but at the improbably fortuitous meeting in the glade of Theseus, Palamon, and Arcite, described in the lines that immediately follow (1.1683–713). This encounter is one of many features in the first half of the tale that show that most of the plot, far from being the product of portentous cosmic forces (Palamon and Arcite are consistently made to look silly for taking this view), is generated by human actions and choices, not least by those of the narrating Knight in conspicuously rigging events and manipulating coincidences. The Knight, as Neuse points out, is adapting an "olde storie" for the present occasion, and the irony here reflects his opinion of the style of those "olde bookes." To him that style embodies a dangerous evasion of human responsibility for maintaining order in self and society by unconsciously projecting the responsibility onto gods and destinies.

The point is that a notion like "unimpersonated artistry," by dividing speakers into parts and denying them the full import of their speaking, puts us in the difficult position of trying to decide which parts of a single narrative are to be assigned to the pilgrim teller and which to the "author," and in these circumstances it is not surprising that different critics make the cut in different places. All such formulations involve finding or creating two speakers (or even more) in a narrative situation where it would appear simpler to deal with only one. The procedure seems to me theoretically questionable because it is unparsimonious or inelegant logically: it creates extra work, and it also tends to lead to distraction. Narrative entities are multiplied to the point where they become subjects of concern in their own right and require some sort of systematic or historical justification such as "unimpersonated artistry" or the deficiency of medieval ideas of personality, and before long we are so busy trying to save the appearances of the epicyclic constructs we ourselves have created that we are no longer attending to the poems that the constructs were originally intended to explain. Therefore, I would like to preface my more detailed opposition to "unimpersonated artistry" with a general caveat. I call it Leicester's razor: "narratores non multiplicandi sunt praeter absolutum necessitatem."

Naturally I do not intend to let the matter rest with this general and essentially negative formula, though I think its application would clear up a lot of difficulties. I want to use the space my principle gives me to argue that the Canterbury tales are individually voiced, and radically so—that each of the tales is primarily an expression of its teller's personality and outlook as embodied in the unfolding "now" of the telling. I am aware that something like this idea is all too familiar. Going back, in modern times, at least as far as Kittredge's characterization of the *Canterbury Tales* as a "Human Comedy," with the pilgrims as dramatis personae, it reaches its high point in Lumiansky's *Of Sondry Folk* (and apparently its dead end as well, since no one since has attempted to apply the concept systematically to the entire poem). Moreover, as I said before, we are all given to this sort of reading now and then. I think one reason the idea has never been pushed so hard or so far as I would like to take it is that the voicing of individual tales has almost always been interpreted on the basis of something external to them, usually either some aspect of the historical background of the poems (e.g., what we know from other sources about knights, millers, lawyers, nuns, etc.) or the descriptions of the speakers given in the Canterbury frame, especially in the General Prologue. Such materials are combined in various ways to construct an image of a given pilgrim outside his or her tale, and each tale is then read as a product of the figure who tells it, a product whose interpretation is constrained by the limitations we conceive the pilgrim to have. The specific problem of historical presuppositions, the feeling that medieval men *could not* have thought or spoken in certain ways, I would like to postpone until later, because the assumptions involved are often relatively tacit and well hidden and the problems they present are easier to handle in specific instances. It is clear, I hope, how such assumptions can lead to the kind of constraint on interpretation I have just outlined and how such a constraint puts us in danger of arguing from inference back to evidence, in Robert O. Payne's useful phrase, when what is desired is an understanding of the evidence—the text—in front of us (*The Key of Remembrance: A Study of Chaucer's Poetics*).

It is the specific problem of the Canterbury frame, however, that has been the more stubborn obstacle to reading the tales as examples of impersonated artistry. Since I do not mean by this phrase what either the critics or the defenders of similar notions appear to have meant in the past, the topic is worth pausing over. The issue is generally joined over the question of verisimilitude, the consistency with which the fiction of the *Tales* can be felt to sustain a dramatic illusion of real people taking part in real and present interaction with one another. The critic who has most consistently taken this dramatic view of the poem is Lumiansky, who locates both the "reality" of the pilgrims and the "drama" of their relations with one another outside the tales themselves, preeminently in the frame. He ordinarily begins his discussion of a given tale and its dramatic context with a character sketch of the pilgrim drawn from the General Prologue (and from any relevant links) and then treats the tale itself as an exemplification and extension of the traits and situations in the frame. He is attentive to such details as direct addresses to the pilgrim audience within a tale (such as the Knight's "lat se now who shal the soper wynne") and to a degree to the ways tales respond to one another, as in fragment 3, or the Marriage Group. This approach leads to an account of the poem as a whole that doubles the overt narrative of the frame and, in effect, allows the frame to tyrannize the individual tales: what does not fit the model of actual, preexisting pilgrims really present to one another is not relevant to the enterprise and is variously ignored or dismissed. Other critics have not been slow to point out that this procedure neglects a great deal.

The objection to this "dramatic" model that I would particularly like to single out is its disregard for the poem's insistent, though perhaps intermittent, *textuality,* for the way the work repeatedly breaks the fiction of spoken discourse and the illusion of the frame to call attention to itself as a written thing. The injunction in the Miller's Prologue to "turne over the leef and chese another tale" (1.3177), the more interesting moment in the Knight's Tale when the supposedly oral narrator remarks, "But of that storie list me nat to write" (1.1201)—such interruptions not only destroy "verisimilitude" but call attention to what Howard has named the "bookness" of the poem (*Idea*), as do, less vibrantly, incipits and explicits, the patently incomplete state of the text, or "the contingency that a tale not memorized but told impromptu is in verse." Now this conspicuous textuality (by which I mean that Chaucer not only produces written texts but does so self-consciously and calls attention to his writing) certainly militates strongly against the illusion of drama as living presence. It is no doubt this realization, coupled with the counterperception that some tales do seem "fitted to the teller," that has led Howard and others to adopt formulations like "unimpersonated artistry" in order to stay responsive to the apparent range of the poem's effects. Such a notion allows the critic to hover between "bookness," which the French have taught us always implies *absence,* and what Howard calls "voiceness": the *presence* we feel when "the author addresses us directly and himself rehearses tales told aloud by others: we seem to hear his and the pilgrim's voices, we presume oral delivery" (*Idea*). If we cannot have presence fully, we can at least have it partly. But when and where exactly and, above all, *whose?* As I have tried to suggest, a phenomenon like "unimpersonated artistry"—which is, remember, an *intermittent* phenomenon—tries to save the feeling that someone is present at the cost of rendering us permanently uncertain about who is speaking at any given moment in (or of) the text: the pilgrim, the poet, or that interesting mediate entity Chaucer the pilgrim.

It seems to me that the "roadside-drama" approach, the critiques of this approach, *and* compromise positions (whether explicitly worked out like Howard's or more intuitive) have in common a central confusion: the confusion of *voice* with *presence*. All these views demand that the voice in a text be traceable to a person, a subject, *behind* the language, an individual controlling and limiting, and thereby guaranteeing, the meaning of what is expressed. The language of a given tale, or indeed of a given moment in a tale, is thus the end point of the speaker's activity, the point at which the speaker delivers a self that existed prior to the text. For this reason all these approaches keep circling back to the ambiguous traces of such an external subject—in the frame, in the poet, in the facts of history, or in the "medieval mind." But what I mean by "impersonated artistry" does not involve an external subject.

In maintaining that the *Canterbury Tales* is a collection of individually voiced texts, I want rather to *begin* with the fact of their textuality, to insist that there is nobody there, that there is only the text. But if a written text implies and enforces the absence of the subject, the real living person outside the text who may or may not have "expressed himself" in producing it, the same absence is emphatically *not* true of the voice *in* the text, the voice *of* the text. In writing, voice is first of all a function not of persons but of language, of the linguistic codes and conventions that make it *possible* for an "I" to appear. But this possibility means that we can assign an "I" to any statement. Language is positional. It always states or implies a first person in potential dramatic relation to the other grammatical persons, and it does so structurally—qua language—and regardless of the presence or absence of any actual speaking person. Thus, by its nature as a linguistic phenomenon, any text generates what it is conventional to call its speaker. The speaker is created by the text itself as a structure of linguistic relationships, and the character of the speaker is a function of the specific deployment of those relationships in a particular case to produce the voice of the text.

This kind of "voiceness" is a property of any text, and it is therefore theoretically possible to read any text in a way that elicits its particular voice, its individual first person. Such a reading would, for example, try to attend consistently to the "I" of the text, expressed or implied, and would make the referential aspects of the discourse functions of the "I." To put it another way, a voice-oriented reading would treat the second and third persons of a discourse (respectively, the audience and the world), expressed or implied, primarily as indications of what the speaker *maintains* about audience and world and would examine the way these elements are reflexively constituted as evidence of the speaker's character. We would ask what sort of person notices these particular details rather than others, what sort of person conceives of an audience in such a way that he or she addresses it in this particular tone, and so forth.

One might conceive of a study that undertook to work out a poetics of the speaker in literature. It would be a classic structuralist enterprise, moving from linguistic structures to a systematic demonstration of how it is possible for literary speakers to have the meanings they do. But since I do not believe, for reasons I will not go into here, that such an enterprise would succeed, and since in any case it is not where my interests lie, I would like to move back to Chaucer by way of a further distinction. While any text can be read in a way that elicits its voice, some texts actively engage the phenomenon of voice, exploit it, make it the center of their discourse—make it their content. A text of this sort can be said to be *about* its speaker, and this is the sort of text I contend that the *Canterbury Tales* is and especially the sort that the individual tales are. The tales are examples of impersonated artistry because they concentrate not on the way preexisting people create language but on the way language creates people. They detail how what someone says "im-personates" him or her, that is, turns the speaker into a person, or better, a personality (I prefer this word to "person" because "personality" suggests something that acts like, rather than "is," a person). What this implies for the concrete interpretation of the poem is that the relation that I have been questioning between the tales and the frame, or between the tales and their historical or social background, needs to be reversed. The voicing of any tale, the personality of any pilgrim, is not *given* in advance by the prologue portrait or the facts of history, nor is it dependent on them. The personality has to be worked out by analyzing and defining the voice created by each tale. It is this personality in the foreground, in his or her intensive and detailed textual life, that supplies a guide to the weighting of details and emphasis, the *interpretation*, of the background, whether portrait or history. To say, for example, that the Miller's Tale is not "fitted to its teller" because it is "too good" for him, because a miller or the Miller would not be educated enough or intelligent enough to produce it, is to move in exactly the wrong direction. In fact, it is just this sort of social typing that irritates and troubles the Miller himself, especially since both the Host and the general narrator social-typed him long before any Chaucer critic did (1.3128–31, 3167–69, 3182). The characters in his tale repeatedly indulge in social typing, and the Miller types several of them in this way. The Miller's handling of this practice makes it an issue in the tale, something he has opinions and feelings about. The end of the tale makes it quite clear how the maimed, uncomfortably sympathetic carpenter is sacrificed to the mirth of the townsfolk and the pilgrims; he is shouted down by the class solidarity of Nicholas' brethren: "For every clerk anonright heeld with oother" (1.3847). One could go on to show how the Miller's sensibility in the tale retrospectively and decisively inflects the portrait of him in the General Prologue, making it something quite different from what it appears to be in prospect, but the same point can be suggested more economically with the Physician. When we read in the Prologue that "His studie was but litel on the Bible" (1.438), the line sounds condemnatory in an absolute, moral way. Reconsidered from the perspective of the tale, however, the detail takes on a new and more intensive individual life in the light of the Physician's singularly inept use of the exemplum of Jephthah's daughter (6.238–50). Retrospectively the poet's comment characterizes a man of irreproachable if conventional morality whose profession channels his reading into medical texts rather than sacred ones and who uses such biblical knowledge as he has for pathetic effect at the expense of narrative consistency: he forgets, or at any rate suppresses, that Jephthah's daughter asked for time to bewail her virginity, whereas Virginia is being killed to preserve hers. The situation in the tale is a good deal more complex than this, but I think the general point is clear enough: it is the tale that specifies the portrait, not the other way around.

The technique of impersonation as I am considering it here has no necessary connection whatever with the question of the integration of a given tale in the Canterbury frame. The Knight's mention of writing in his tale is indeed an anomalous detail in the context of the pilgrimage. It is often regarded as a sign of the incomplete revision of the (hypothetical) "Palamon and Arcite," supposedly written before Chaucer had the idea of the *Tales* and afterward inserted in its present position in fragment 1. The reference to writing is taken as evidence that the Knight was not the "original" speaker and, in a reading like Howard's, that he is still not always the speaker. As far as it goes, the argument about the chronology of composition is doubtless valid, but it has nothing to do with the question of whether or not the tale is impersonated, a question that can, and ought to, be separated, at least initially, from the fiction of the pilgrimage. Details like the Knight's "write" are not immediately relevant because they do not affect the intention to create a speaker (they may become relevant at a different level of analysis later). Impersonation, the controlled use of voicing to direct us to what a narrative tells us about its narrator, *precedes dramatization of the Canterbury sort* in Chaucer, analytically and no doubt sometimes chronologically. The proper method is to ascribe the entire narration in all its details to a *single* speaker (on the authority of Leicester's razor) and to use it as evidence in constructing that speaker's consciousness, keeping the question of the speaker's "identity" open until the analysis is complete. It is convenient and harmless to accept the frame's statement that the Knight's Tale is "the tale the Knight tells" as long as we recognize that it merely gives us something to call the speaker and tells us nothing reliable about him in advance.

I want to conclude an already perverse argument with a further perversity. I have argued that we ought to reverse the ordinary commonsense approach to the relations between foreground and background in the poem and see the pilgrims as the products rather than as the producers of their tales. I have suggested further that Chaucer's fiction may explain, rather than be explained by, the facts of fourteenth-century social history. I now want to maintain that the poet is the creation rather than the creator of his poem. More perversely still, I want to put a nick in my own razor and reintroduce a version of the double narrator in Chaucer. I do this in order to question a notion more widespread and apparently more durable than the various versions of "unimpersonated artisty," the notion of Chaucer the pilgrim. I must admit to being less sure of my ground here. For one thing, I am challenging an idea first put forward by E. Talbot Donaldson, who has for years been producing the best line-by-line interpretations of Chaucer that I know, using what amounts to the very technique of reading I have been urging here.

Nevertheless, it seems clear on the face of it that issues of the sort I have been discussing are raised by the notion of Chaucer the pilgrim, the naïve narrator of the General Prologue and the links, who so often misses the point of the complex phenomena he describes in order that Chaucer the satirist or the poet or the man can make sure *we* see how very complex they are. The idea leads to a multiplication of speakers of the same text, not serially (though some critics have considered this possibility too), but simultaneously. It requires that in any given passage we first decide what Chaucer the pilgrim means by what he says and then what Chaucer the poet means by what the pilgrim means. Here, too, there is often confusion about the distinction between the voice of the text and a presence behind and beyond it who somehow guarantees the meaning we find there. Descriptions of Chaucer the poet sometimes take on a distinctly metaphysical cast, as in this passage from Donaldson's *Speaking of Chaucer:*

> Undoubtedly Chaucer the man would, like his fictional representative, have found [the Prioress] charming and looked on her

> with affection. To have got on so well in so changeable a world Chaucer must have got on well with the people in it, and it is doubtful that one may get on with people merely by pretending to like them: one's heart has to be in it. But the third entity, Chaucer the poet, operates in a realm which is above and subsumes those in which Chaucer the man and Chaucer the pilgrim have their being. In this realm prioresses may be simultaneously evaluated as marvellously amiable ladies and as prioresses.

But the "higher realm" Donaldson is talking about is and can only be the *poem,* the text—as he himself knows perfectly well—and Chaucer the poet can only be what I have been calling the voice of the text. Donaldson is, as always, attentive to what the text *says* here, in particular to the tensions among social, human, and moral elements that the General Prologue undeniably displays. The division of the speaker into pilgrim, man, and poet is a way of registering these tensions and their complexity, of suggesting "a vision of the social world imposed on one of the moral world," and I can have no objection to this aim. I do not see the need, however, to reify these tensions into separate personalities of the same speaker, and I think this way of talking about the narrator of the General Prologue is misleading because it encourages us to treat him *as if we knew who he was* apart from his utterances. The general personality traits of Chaucer the pilgrim have themselves become reified in the Chaucer criticism of the last twenty years, and this frozen concept of the character has fostered a carelessness in reading that Donaldson himself rarely commits.

If I were going to try to characterize the speaker of the General Prologue myself, I would follow the lead of John M. Major in calling him, not naïve, but extraordinarily sophisticated. I doubt, however, that this characterization, even if accepted, would go very far toward solving the problems of the poem, because it still does not tell us much about who the speaker is, and that is what we want to know. The notion of Chaucer the pilgrim at least offers us an *homme moyen sensuel* with whom we can feel we know where we are, but I think that it is just this sense of knowing where we are, with whom we are dealing, that the General Prologue deliberately and calculatedly denies us. For a brief suggestion of this intention—which is all I can offer here—consider these lines from the Monk's portrait, a notorious locus for the naïveté of the narrator:

> He yaf nat of that text a pulled hen,
> That seith that hunters ben nat hooly men.
> Ne that a monk, whan he is recchelees.

Is likned til a fissh that is waterlees,—
This is to seyn, a monk out of his cloystre.
But thilke texte heeld he nat worth an oystre;
And I seyde his opinion was good.
What sholde he studie and make hymselven wood,
Upon a book in cloystre alwey to poure,
Or swynken with his handes, and laboure,
As Austyn bit? How shal the world be served?
Lat Austyn have his swynk to hym reserved!
Therfore he was a prikasour aright.

(1.177–89)

The Monk's own bluff manner is present in these lines. I agree with most commentators that he is being half-quoted, that we hear his style, for example, in the turn of a phrase like "nat worth an oystre!" Present too are the standards of his calling, against which, if we will, he may be measured. The social and moral worlds do indeed display their tension here, but who brought these issues up? Who is responsible for the slightly suspended enjambment that turns "As Austyn bit?" into a small firecracker? For the wicked specificity with which, at the beginning of the portrait, the Monk's bridle is said to jingle "as dooth the *chapel* belle"? Who goes to such pains to explain the precise application of the proverb about the fish, "This is to seyn"? Who if not the speaker? But these observations do not permit us to say that he is *only* making a moral judgment or only making fun of the Monk (the two are not quite the same, and both are going on). A sense of the positive claims made by the pilgrim's vitality, his "manliness," is also registered by the portrait. The speaker's amused enjoyment of the Monk's forthright humanity is too patent to let us see him as just a moralist. The way his voice evokes complex possibilities of attitude is neatly caught by "And I seyde his opinion was good": that's what he said when he and the Monk had their conversation, but is he saying the same thing now in this portrait? Did he really mean it at the time? Does he now? In what sense?

The point of this exercise is not merely to show that the speaker's attitude is complex and sophisticated but also to stress how obliquely expressed it is, all in ironic juxtapositions and loaded words whose precise heft is hard to weigh. What we have, in fact, is a speaker who is not giving too much of himself away, who is not telling us, any more than he told the Monk, his whole mind in plain terms. The tensions among social, moral, and existential worlds are embodied in a single voice here, and they are embodied precisely *as tensions,* not as a resolution or a synthesis, for we cannot tell exactly what the speaker thinks either of the Monk or of conventional morality. What we *can* tell is that we are dealing with a speaker who withholds himself from us, with the traces of a presence that asserts its simultaneous absence. The speaker is present as uncomprehended, as not to be seized all at once in his totality. He *displays his difference* from his externalizations, his speaking, in the very act of externalizing himself. It is this effect, I think, that creates the feeling of "reality" in the text, the sense that there is somebody there. In literature (as in life) the reality of characters is a function of their mystery, of the extent to which we are made to feel that there is more going on in regard to them than we know or can predict. Criseyde is a well-known and well-analyzed example in Chaucer, and I suggest that the general narrator of the *Canterbury Tales* is another. His lack of definition may also explain why he can be taken for Chaucer the pilgrim. Because his identity is a function of what he leaves unspoken—because it is derived from implication, irony, innuendo, the potentialities of meaning and intention that occur in the gaps between observations drawn from radically different realms of discourse—there is a temptation to reduce his uncomfortable indeterminacy by forcing the gaps shut, by spelling out the connections. But suppressing the indeterminacy in this way involves reducing complex meanings to simpler ones. One infers "Chaucer the pilgrim" by ignoring the things the speaker "does not say" (since, after all, he does not *say* them—only suggests) and by insisting that he "means" his statements in only the plainest, most literal sense. Such an interpretation does not fail to recognize that the complexities of meaning are there; it simply assigns them to "the poem" or to "Chaucer the poet," thus producing what I am arguing is a contradiction: the simple and naïve narrator of a complex and sophisticated narration.

In fact, however, not only the General Prologue but the whole of the *Canterbury Tales* works against a quick or easy comprehension of the speaker. It is to suggest how it does so that I am going to reintroduce a sort of double narration. First of all, though, it should be clear that there is only one speaker of the entire poem and that he is also the poem's maker. The conspicuous textuality of the work makes this fact inescapable. It may be that Chaucer would have "corrected" anomalies like the Knight's "But of that storie list me nat to write" and that he would have supplied a complete and self-consistent set of links between the present fragments to round out the Canterbury fiction. It seems much less likely that he would have revised the Man of Law's promise to tell his rime-royal tale in prose or the "quod she" in the middle of the Prioress's Tale or the "turne over the leef" passage in the Miller's Prologue or the inordinate and undramatic length of the Melibee. And I am quite certain that he would not have altered the fundamental "contingency that a tale not memorized but told impromptu is in verse." What is at issue here is not simply a neutral medium that we are entitled to ignore. If pentameter couplets are the *koiné* of the poem, stanzaic verse (especially rime royal but also the Monk's stanza and even Sir Thopas's tail rhyme) functions as a formal equivalent, a translation into writing, of a different level of diction: it identifies a speaker with pretensions to an elevated style, in life as well as in storytelling. If it is functional in the poem that one kind of verse be sensed as verse, why not other kinds, and prose as well? The poem's insistence on these distinctions has interesting implications for the problem of oral delivery. The *Canterbury Tales* is not written to be spoken as if it were a play. It is written to be read, but read *as if* it were spoken. The poem is a literary imitation of oral performance.

One effect of this fundamental textuality is to keep us constantly aware that the frame, the reportage, is a patent fiction. There is no pilgrimage, there are no pilgrims. Whether or not Chaucer ever went to Canterbury, whether or not the characters in the poem are drawn from "real life," what we have in front of us is the activity of a poet, a maker, giving his own rhythm and pattern, his own shape and voice, his own complex interpretation to the materials of the poem. And that maker *is the speaker of the poem,* the voice of the text. There is no one there but that voice, that text. The narrator of the *Canterbury Tales* is the speaker we call Chaucer the poet, though it would be more accurate—I cannot resist, this once—to call him Chaucer the poem.

This being said, it is also true that one of the first discoveries we make when we try to characterize this maker and speaker on the evidence of his discourse, to begin to specify the voice of the text, is that he is an impersonator in the conventional sense: he puts fictional others between himself and us. This is the sense in which the tales are double-voiced: each of them is Chaucer impersonating a pilgrim, the narrator speaking in the voice of the Knight or the Reeve or the Second Nun. They are his creatures, voices that he assumes; he gives them his life.

But it would be as accurate, from another perspective, to say that he takes his life from them, and the amount of time and effort spent on making the pilgrims independent, the sheer labor of consistent, unbroken impersonation to which the poem testifies, suggests that this is the more compelling perspective, for Chaucer as for us. The enterprise of the poem involves the continual attempt, continually repeated, to see from another's point of view, to stretch and extend the self by learning to speak in the voices of others; and the poem itself is, among other things, the record of that attempt.

I have tried to evoke, however briefly, the incompleteness—the indeterminacy and the resistance to classification—of the voice that speaks in the General Prologue. One corollary of this quality is the cognate incompleteness of the Prologue itself, one of whose principal themes is the insufficiency of traditional social and moral classifying schemes—estates, hierarchies, and the like—to deal with the complexity of individuals and their relations. The speaker not only embodies this insufficiency, he recognizes it and feels it: "Also I prey yow to foryeve it me, / Al have I nat set folk in hir degree / Heere in this tale, as that they sholde stonde" (1.743–45). From this insufficiency he turns to the pilgrims. He sets them free to speak in part to free himself from the constraints and uncertainties generated by his own attempt to classify them—an attempt that, however universal and impersonal it may look at the beginning of the Prologue, is always only his view and one too complex for him to speak by himself. The Prologue does not do justice to the pilgrims. By the same token and for the same reasons it does not do justice to the narrator and his understanding of his world. In the tales, therefore, he slows us down, keeps us from grasping him too quickly and easily, by directing our attention to the variety and complexity of the roles he plays, the voices he assumes. He is, we know, each of the pilgrims and all of them, but he seems to insist that we can only discover him by discovering for ourselves who the Knight is, who the Parson, who the Pardoner and the Wife of Bath.

We may be impatient to know the speaker of the General Prologue, but as the voice of the poem as a whole, he is the last of the pilgrims we may hope to comprehend, and then only by grasping each of the others individually and in turn and in all the complexity of their relationships to one another. The relation of the voice that speaks in the General Prologue to the personality of the poet is like that of an individual portrait to its tale and that of the Prologue itself to all the tales. It is a prologal voice, a voice that is only beginning to speak. Chaucer's Prologue, like this prologue of mine, needs the tales to fulfill itself in the gradual and measured but always contingent and uncertain activity of impersonation, in both senses. The speaker of the *Canterbury Tales*—Chaucer—is indeed as fictional as the pilgrims, in the sense that like them he is a self-constructing voice. He practices what I have called the art of impersonation, finally, to impersonate himself, to create himself as fully as he can in his work.

The Canterbury Tales as Framed Narratives

Morton W. Bloomfield

Robert Jordan in his interesting book has made the point that "the *Canterbury Tales* . . . invites piecemeal criticism; it also invites the total view. In the equality of these two claims on our attention lies much of the critical problem." Jordan tends to see the historical explanation of this paradox in the Gothic nature of Chaucer's art, the dominant aesthetic mood of the period, wherein "the total form is determined by the accumulation of individually complete elements." The whole can be regarded as a collection of complete parts which involve varying perspectives and unusual juxtapositions, the very opposite of modern "organic" art wherein the parts are at least theoretically subordinate to the whole.

Although I think that the notion of modern art as organic must be qualified and questioned, there is a certain force and validity to Jordan's distinction between medieval and modern art. Modern art expects the parts to be somewhat subordinate to the whole. The dominant stress of New Criticism was on the organic nature of art. This principle applies mainly to certain poets and novelists of the Renaissance and later periods but certainly not to all. The Victorian novelists did not write organically. Many of the eighteenth-century poets did not. On the other hand, some medieval literature is organic—*Gawain and the Green Knight,* for instance, and some of Chaucer. We do not, therefore, have to relate the individual Canterbury tales to the frame in any psychological, symbolic, or dramatic manner, but we can treat them as separate units. We can look at the frame separately as

From *Leeds Studies in English* n.s. 14 (1983). © 1983 by School of English, University of Leeds.

at another part of the poem, as well as a unifying device. We need not be concerned with the dramatic unity of the *Canterbury Tales*. I do not, however, deny that some relation even if not an organic one, exists between the frame and the tales. The former is at least causative and authenticating. As we shall see, it provides the narrative cause for the other narratives, and it attempts to authenticate the stories, that is, to help make the reader or audience suspend their disbelief. This is the usual procedure in most collections of tales. We shall here examine the rather complex background of the frame and its numerous aesthetic functions to see what light this knowledge may throw on Chaucer's general intention. It may help us to learn how Chaucer himself regarded his great masterpiece.

There is a sense, it must, however, be acknowledged, in which the tales—or most of them—are also reflections of their tellers, and this relationship adds another dimension to their complexity of perspective and meaning. This aspect has, however, been much overstressed by early twentieth-century criticism, an emphasizing which has blurred the structure of the units in their own right. Chaucer is a great psychologist, but he was not the exclusive psychologist-realist and prober of the human heart that modern critics and scholars prodded by early twentieth-century interests have made him out to be. Modern criticism, with its strong mimetic bias, has tended to emphasize character and dramatic incident at the expense of structure and sequence, and it is time to redress somewhat the balance. Chaucer was influenced by the literary and rhetorical tradition as much as by life.

There were many possible precedents for a collection of tales more or less unified in some way, and before we proceed further we should glance briefly at some of these collections. As Nevill Coghill has pointed out, Chaucer's idea of a collection was novel and original, but he could also have been indebted to predecessors. He certainly would have relied in some way, no matter how original his idea was, on the tradition of a collection of tales to interest readers. We must then look at several possible exemplars.

Before we go into some detail, it is important to note the religious and moral suggestions which a collection of tales would connote to readers in fourteenth-century England. Not all of Chaucer's models are religious, but the really popular collections of tales had a didactic purpose. Collections of saints' lives, of fables, of miracles of the virgin, and of exempla for sermons certainly provided the fundamental exemplars for Chaucer and even Boccaccio. These collections had a practical purpose and came into existence for the convenience of religious teachers.

I do not wish to deny that early secular collections like *The Seven Sages* and other Oriental collections may have influenced Chaucer in some way. I think, however, the English audience, even a court audience, would have normally expected a didactic and religious purpose in any collection of tales presented to them inasmuch as these didactic assemblages were the most common type of narrative collections in the period.

The twelfth century for the first time in the West saw the development of collections of tales, tales primarily for the convenience of preaching and devotional purposes. The earlier collections such as the *Vitae patrum* and some hagiographic collections were essentially for monks, making provision for communal and spiritual readings in the monastery. The Moslem world, though these were mainly secular and entertaining, did have collected and framed tales dating from before the twelfth century—notably the *Arabian Nights* (in some of its forms) and *The Seven Sages*. Among Oriental fable collections the Arabic *Kalilah and Dimnah* or *Fables of Bidpai* are also of early date. Nevertheless *The Seven Sages* and *Kalilah* were not translated into Western languages before the twelfth century. Aesopic collections made in classical times and Ovid's *Metamorphoses* were, however, known. The latter at the beginning of book 4 even has three daughters of King Minyas carry on discussions between their tales.

The great upsurge in collections dating from the twelfth and thirteenth centuries is due, as might be expected, to a demand for moralizing stories as literate and religious audiences increased in size. Collections of tales were useful for preaching friars who turned increasingly to sermons to win over urban audiences. Stories and anecdotes have always been used in teaching but the notion of an organized collection of such, if not new in the West, at least received a new attention. The later Middle Ages is a great period of collected stories—the legends of the Virgin began to appear in the twelfth century, and proliferated until the Reformation; exempla books are very numerous indeed in the same period; great legendaries, especially Jacob of Voragine's *Golden Legend,* flourish; even works on other subjects, like Peraldus's *Summa virtutum et vitiorum,* are infiltrated by exempla; older collections like those of Valerius Maximus and the *Vitae patrum* take on, as their MSS show, a new life in this period. We also find collections of a *De casibus* type wherein tragedies or strictly speaking falls are told, or of a *De illustribus* type wherein brief biographical lists of great people are provided.

It is possible that the Gothic spirit was responsible in part for the efflorescence of an older genre, but there is probably a more prosaic reason at the bottom—sheer convenience. These collections were useful for preachers. The authorities on preaching emphasize the importance of illustrating homiletic points by concrete stories. There is perhaps no "clear-cut treatment of the exemplum" in the *Artes predicandi,* those rhetoric books for preachers, but that its use was strongly urged there can be no doubt.

This passion for collecting also extended to anthologies of poetry and dictionaries of various sorts. Traditionally, in the medieval period, we find classical poetry introduced by the *accessus ad auctores* in which the circumstances of the composition of the work presented are often given, sometimes in terms of four Aristotelian causes. St. Jerome applied what the *Rhetorica ad Herennium* and Cicero's *De inventione* has recommended, an introduction to the beginning of each of his commentaries on the books of the Bible he translated. His example was very influential. We sometimes find brief biographies embedded in *accessus.* Medieval literary history was conceived of as introductions to particular literary works. This passion extended to the Provencal *razos,* discussions of the external circumstances of composition of poems preceding them in a number of Provencal manuscripts. These are also *accessus* of a sort. Biographies of these poets, usually separate from the *razos,* abound. The Prologue to *Canterbury Tales,* if not all parts of the frame, can be regarded in part as an *accessus.* It exists in part to describe the fictitious authors and the "causes" of the tales themselves.

A distinction should be made between collections of tales with a prologue from the author as a real person and framed tales with a prologue which is also a fiction and which may have, as the *Decameron* and *Canterbury Tales* do, framing interludes. The *accessus* is from the author as a real person. The Prologue to the *Canterbury Tales* is an artistic, made-up *accessus,* not a real one.

A frame, besides justifying the tales or collected stories, also exists for authenticating purposes. Most stories pretend to be real, to be "historical" in some sense. Part of the pleasure of a story for a reader or hearer lies in the suspension of disbelief engendered by the claim, open or implied, that the story is true. If the magic of art is to work, it must be true. This feeling that what is told really happened is a very old tradition, almost certainly going back to early oral societies. The host when he describes the Canterbury scheme says that each pilgrim will tell four tales "of aventures that whilom han bifalle" (1. 795; F. N. Robinson, 2d ed.), each tale to be about things and matters which really happened. One of the major purposes of the frame, then, is to authenticate the tales—to play the game that the stories are real. Here, as I have elsewhere written, "Chaucer has moved from dream and past history [in his earlier poetry] to a report on the contemporary world and present history. . . . We are given a social world in the frame, not an individual's problems or attitudes." The "realism" of the *Canterbury Tales* which lies in great measure in the frame rather than the tales themselves, however, does not arise out of a desire to give us a "true" picture of fourteenth-century life as a medieval Zola might wish to do but to an important degree out of a well-known literary purpose—authentication. The attempt to show the truth of a tale; "it really happened," is its indirect theme. Besides this aim, the genre of collected tales—not only the Gothic spirit—demanded a prologue and sometimes a total frame.

Then, further, the frame is in the form of a supposititious pilgrimage to St. Thomas's shrine in Canterbury. This imagery suggests, on a literary level, the pilgrim's report, which is told in the first person, presumably of a personal experience. The pilgrimage notion, besides its obvious religious symbolism, serves as a literary authenticating device for the Chaucer persona. We are all pilgrims on the way to our different Canterburys. Life is a journey to our final homes; and besides, this governing image helps us to suspend our disbelief and listen to a pilgrim's tale, of one who has just made a voyage. A good more or less contemporary report in English is that of Margery Kempe who, in her *Autobiography,* tells *inter alia* of her journey to Palestine in Chaucer's period. Most pilgrim's tales are in Latin, but by Chaucer's time, vernacular reports were beginning to appear.

It is also significant for the understanding of the framed tales of the period that the single-centered narrative of early Arthurian romance began to give way in the thirteenth century and even more in the fourteenth to the Arthurian prose cycle type of narrative which is formed by rambling disgressions having a common Arthurian background but introducing a vast number of what seem to and may actually be irrelevant stories. The story within the story goes wild and multiplies in a bewildering way. The collections as well as the *Canterbury Tales* are held together by a recognizable purpose or plan, the prose cycles are not. Yet the urge to proliferate tales is there and may also be explained by this later medieval drive to create collections. It is so urgent that Chaucer makes one of his tales, the Monk's Tale, a smaller collection of tales—"little tragedies"—within a larger collection.

All this may be seen in some great late medieval collections. In the fourteenth century, three remarkable men, Juan Ruiz in Spain, Boccaccio in Italy, and Chaucer in England, took the religious or moralizing genre of collected tales and infused it with new life and vitality in a way that few early secular collections were able to be animated. This is not the place to go into a detailed comparison, but each author had a complex artistic vision, and however different in aims and form produced masterpieces. They diversified their narratives by "retrospection and anticipation," and by subtle shifts in perspective they gave us several worlds held together in a most subtle articulation.

None of Chaucer's predecessors, however, use exactly his device. Nor does any combine the religious and secular attitudes and subjects to the degree he does. Chaucer gives us a spiritual vision both directly and indirectly.

The *Decameron* has no interludes except at the beginning of the whole work and between days. As Robert Pratt and Karl Young point out, "it is clear that the frame of the *Decameron* could not be regarded as Chaucer's model in any precise or thorough-going sense." (See *Sources and Analogues of Chaucer's* Canterbury Tales, ed. W. F. Bryan and Germaine Dempster.) The *Ameto* and *Filocolo,* both by Boccaccio, especially the *Ameto,* are somewhat closer to the *Canterbury Tales* but even they differ from the latter in significant ways. Sercambi, whose collection of tales used to be considered the closest Italian source of or analogue to the *Canterbury Tales,* now seems out of the running because of a correction in his assumed dates. The *Libro del buen amor* is even less like the *Canterbury Tales* than the Italian examples I have named. We must not forget, of course, Ovid's great collection of tales, especially because Ovid was so popular in the later Middle Ages, but the *Metamorphoses* is fundamentally different in structure from the *Canterbury Tales.*

Art traditionally teaches and amuses. These three masterpieces, the *Libro del buen amor,* the *Decameron,* and the *Canterbury Tales,* stress these two aims differently. Chaucer teaches most of all. They all make some use of circumstantial realism for literary ends, but they are all pictures of life only in the most profound sense. They are also partly true to life because the religious tradition out of which they come is true of life. The sermons and penitential books of the Christian tradition are realistic.

Chaucer's notions of dialogue and the elaboration of the role of the persona are too varied in origin to trace here, but they no doubt are part of the complex sense of the world which Chaucer delighted in. Wyclif, Chaucer's great contemporary, said that "pulcra alternacio delectat animam" and that "multi delectantur in loquela dialogi." Chaucer knew too that debate and dialogue delighted and soul. Many of the religious collections of tales had prefaces, but they were written by the author as author, commenting on his collection, praising God and possibly offering reasons and uses for the tales that follow. What Ruiz, Boccaccio, and Chaucer did was to make the prologues and frames linking the tales part of the artistic creation (a very rare device indeed in religious collections, and usually confined to titles). The tales themselves were pushed to a secondary level so to speak. The prologue and framing links became the setting out of which the tales came. Neither Ruiz nor Boccaccio used the links in as complete a way as nor to the same extent that Chaucer did. An imitation of reality, not an opinion of the author or presumed author speaking in his own person, provided, however, the rationale of the collection for all three.

Chaucer and his Mediterranean colleagues used circumstantial detail of time, place and description in their prologues and frames, and following an old tradition, descriptions of characters and lively dialogue. The circumstantial detail of the frame we have already discussed elsewhere. It is especially presented for its purpose in authenticating. The portrait goes back to the classical world as a literary genre and was recommended by medieval writers on rhetoric and poetics. Dialogue was considered, as we have seen, a proper form for medieval writers to use to increase the delectation of their audiences.

In making something of this genre, these writers then used dialogue, debate, and circumstantial realism to make a complex perspectivism and a rich, ironical, self-aware sense of life. Each was a maker of a world or worlds. Each "thickened the mixture" and made their audience see the bitter-sweetness of existence.

The frame of the *Canterbury Tales* serves many functions and is not there, as some think, only to serve as an introduction to some attractive tales. It sets the tone for the richness and complexity of human experience presented to us. It authenticates, prepares us for morality and entertainment in various subtle ways. It offers another level of experience, another world out of which the ideal, that is the unreal, world of the tales come. It introduces us to characters of extraordinary range; it universalizes, in a religious sense, the stories; it satisfies the Gothic urge for wholes within wholes; it gives a sense of completeness and plenitude such as suggests on a very small scale God's activity within the world. The practical purposes of an introduction to stories are there, of course, but above all a real act of creation is suggested in which a new world appears made out of the stuff of the old.

The spring setting of the Prologue continues the notion of creation, for God was supposed to have created the world in this season. Chaucer, following the medieval rhetoricians, is less concerned with describing spring than with emphasizing its powers (*vires*). The beginning of the poem then suggests creation just as the end suggests the ultimate end of man the pilgrim, and finally of the world. The world of *Canterbury Tales* moves from its own genesis to its final revelation in the Parson's Tale and Chaucer's palinode.

The great character of the frame is the host. He is both the speaker for Chaucer and Chaucer's great critic. He is the supposed creator of the scheme of the tales and is the sole judge of it. He is therefore a Chaucer surrogate and at a great remove a surrogate for God. Yet he lacks complete freedom to impose his will as he quickly learns. God also in a mysterious way is limitied by his creation, but it is a voluntary limitation for man's good.

When Dryden wrote of the *Canterbury Tales* in his *Preface to the Fables,* "Here is God's plenty," he no doubt had the notion of divine plenitude in the back of his mind as an enlightening metaphor, but he builded better than he knew, for the creation (both *natura naturans* and *natura naturata*) of the *Canterbury Tales* with its encompassing and richly variegated frame is really an artistic parallel to God's creation. Traditionally the variety of the world (its plenitude) has always been taken as evidence of God's goodness which overflows into his creation in a variety of ways and manifests itself in as many forms as possible.

Just as secondary causes operate in the world below, all ultimately dependent on God, the primary cause of all, so secondary causes in the forms of Chaucer's many characters create their own stories. But we who observe the whole scene, who read the tales and frame are aware of a mind behind it all, the controlling guide and spirit, to whose goodness we are indebted—Chaucer the man.

As Charles Owen writes, "the embracing fiction [of the pilgrimage] not only gives a value to most of the narratives more important than any they inherently possess, but it manifests itself frequently within the stories influencing their form, their ideology, their style, their language." The Prologue and frame is Chaucer's tribute to and imitation of God's creative activity. Because it is set, unlike Chaucer's other works, in the "real" world, it suggests that we too are characters in a pilgrimage and that we have our little flurries of creation, our narratives as we pass by the way. As Owen has said above, the frame penetrates the stories by creating their form and their rationale. We are both free and determined, masters and slaves, and our lives are the parameters of innumerable variables in a multidimensional continuum.

A further parallel between Chaucer and the Divine is the retrospective stance, the telling of events after they have occurred. As R. Baldwin pointed out a number of years ago, the scheme of the *Canterbury Tales* demands a Chaucer who has already made the journey to Canterbury and is telling it in retrospect. The pilgrim Chaucer as he tells us of the first meeting of his fellow pilgrims describes them fully, something which could only have been done after he had got to know them. The tale of *Canterbury Tales* is being told after the events, even if not in tranquillity. It is cast in the shape of an autobiographical reminiscence. In this, Chaucer is following a very common tradition in art which uses a retrospective teller—perhaps the best known example to him was the *Divine Comedy*. Dante has already completed or pretended to have completed his whole journey as he sits down to relate it to his audience. Paradise has already been reached before Dante the author sits down to write of hell. Chaucer too must have pretended to have reached Canterbury and even to have returned to London before he turned to write

> Whan that Aprill with his shoures soote
> The droghte of March hath perced to the roote.

In at least this sense then the end is the beginning and the beginning is the end in a tale in which the teller is an active character. The motto "En mon commencement est ma fin" and its converse are the truth which Christianity and life give us. This kind of reminiscence then in which the whole work is cast into retrospect is a paradigm again of God's creation and the divine attitude to existence. As in life, the end hovers over every act and all is cast in a perspective of double time. The potential pastness of the present continually being forced upon us by the conditions of this act is what gives the present its edge and its tragedy. We can forget this great truth most of the time, just as we do when we read the tales in the *Canterbury Tales* or as the pilgrims do as they tell their tales, but at times the warning bell clangs as the voice of the narrator, of this elvish man Chaucer, is heard above the clamour in measured tones giving us his report of this journey to Canterbury.

The Prologue and frame then of the *Canterbury Tales* interpenetrate the tales in many and varied ways and set the conditions for the complex worlds which are revealed. The tales are in another time than the time of the pilgrimage for the pilgrimage is given to us in the persona's retrospective time, *in illo tempore*. In a sense the tales then are lyric interludes or perhaps lyrico-narrative interludes, especially because we are strongly aware of most of the tellers. We are held down by the forces which control us, and yet these forces allow each one of us to tell his tale, to open up for a little while the sequence of something that has happened.

Explanations of the function of the Prologue and frame of the *Canterbury Tales* which fall back on the Gothic nature of the late medieval period may to some extent be right. Obviously in some sense the spirit of the later medieval period with its preference for framed painting and framed doorway has some relation to the popularity of the framed collection of tales in the same period and with what Jordan calls "nonorganicist sensibility" so characteristic of Gothic art. Jordan himself is well aware of the difficulties in making precise such parallels. The dispute over whether we can use the term "baroque" or how to use it in discussing seventeenth-century literature is instructive in this matter. Jordan writes, "I do not press the analogy very far."

It is perhaps more helpful in our goal of understanding the function of the frame and Prologue in the *Canterbury Tales* to stress what Chaucer was doing in his concept of the tales; how he conceived his own masterpiece. I think the analogy of creation and God was before him deliberately and often. If we like, we may also interpret Gothic cathedrals thus—remembering though that romanesque and baroque cathedrals also aimed at creating God's house on earth and a replica of the creation and its results in salvation history. It is better to think of Chaucer as a divine surrogate in his task than only as a Gothic artist, though certainly no one can object to these analogies if they are helpful.

The poetic world created by the poet is not really ex nihilo, as Chaucer would surely not wish to put himself on a level with the real God. He is, however, analogously creating a world or several worlds, even if using already existing materials. He is creating, to use an expression of M. H. Abrams, a heterocosm, and is suggesting a parallel to the divine activity. The notion of artist as God is implicit in his greatest poems. The idea of the poet as creator only became explicit in the Renaissance. Yet the poet as *vates,* as prophet who is divinely inspired, is very old, older than Homer. But the notion of the prophet-poet as a god probably had to wait on Christianity and the development of Western thought, especially in the Romantic period.

The idea that the poet is a kind of god is implied in the very subject matter of *The Divine Comedy*. The fact that such a journey should be granted to him as it was to St Paul who visited the third heaven was a sufficient guarantee that Dante was specially favoured and was by precept and example made a special imitation of God, who in the form of Jesus made a journey similar in some respects to what his was to be.

With Chaucer the evidence is less clear but none the less impressive. His characters carry their heavens and hells about with them. They are on their way to the heavenly Jerusalem and are fortuitously joined by Chaucer just as we fortuitously join our own contemporaries at our birth. Chaucer is withdrawn and different. He is called upon by the Host twice, is poked fun at by the Man of Law, tells a dull story. All this gives us a sense of his reality and helps to guarantee his artistic truth. He gives us a world which reflects a real world and in which we find new worlds. It presents its own truth. Its epistemological guarantee is Chaucer's own retrospective report.

We can, if we wish, look upon these two narrative levels—the level of the world of fact and the level of imaginative creation—as an imitation of life itself as it is lived. We live in time punctuated by events which take us out of time, our dreams, some of our contacts with others, our hearing stories, our introspective and imaginative moments. The *Canterbury Tales* reflects these two basic levels of life. It lets us enjoy and lament over our scattered introspective and neighbourly moments as well as keep us aware of the pilgrimage, the *via* we are all bound on. We are the pilgrims, the *viatores,* but just as the Canterbury Pilgrims could get away from their journey carried by the wings of narrative, so we can temporarily forget the serious and fundamental passage to Canterbury we are all engaged upon. The relation between the two levels, then, need not be purely psychological, as Professor Kittredge, Lumiansky, and many others have thought, but religious and humanist.

Thus, the *Canterbury Tales* with its elaborate frame and its Prologue is a prologue to a prologue—our earthly life in its plenitude, variety and multitudinousness. We recognize our world in Chaucer's world and cross in reading it another bridge in "thilke parfit glorious pilgrymage/That highte Jerusalem celestial" (10.50-51).

We must remember that the pilgrims do not reach Canterbury. It is possible that this failure is due to the accident of Chaucer's death or it may be deliberate. I tend to the latter explanation. Chaucer may very well have decided before he reached the Parson's or Manciple's Tale not to finish his work as he had originally planned and reduced it to fewer tales, perhaps even as few as one-quarter of the number. Perhaps not. But the cessation of the work before Canterbury is reached is certainly a happy circumstance or notion in terms of the spiritual function of the Prologue and frame, and the necessity of the return to London. The heavenly Jerusalem is certainly not yet reached by the pilgrims, nor indeed us.

The heavenly Jerusalem is the ultimate goal of earthly man and until the end of time will be for all human beings still *in via*. Even more important, only because more immediate, is the emphasis in the *Canterbury Tales* on the journey of life which all who read it must still be on, with its double aspect of the travelling and the experiences within that journey which seem to take us, even if only momentarily, out of time.

Commercial Language and the Commercial Outlook in the General Prologue

Patricia J. Eberle

One striking feature of the language of the General Prologue to Chaucer's *Canterbury Tales* is the frequent mention of money. References to getting and spending appear repeatedly, not only where we might expect them, for example in the portrait of the worldly Merchant, but also where we might expect any mention of worldly values to be inappropriate, for example in the portraits of the Monk and the Friar, for whom the vow of poverty was at least as important as the vows of chastity and obedience. The portrait of the Monk, however, encludes detailed descriptions of the ways he spends his money, on such luxury items as expensive greyhounds, "for no cost wolde he spare" (l. 192), or on the exquisite grey fur trim on his sleeves, "the fyneste of a lond" (l. 194). If the Monk is remarkable for his virtuosity in spending money, the Friar is equally remarkable for his virtuosity in getting it: "He was the beste beggere in his hous" (l. 252). The Friar has a skill in finding and exploiting commercial opportunities which even the Merchant might envy. Avoiding the poor and cultivating the rich, he seeks out such company as franklins, worthy women, and "selleres of vitaille" (l. 248); this last detail marks the Friar as an astute observer of socioeconomic realities in fourteenth-century London, where the victualling guilds were becoming increasingly powerful, and where one grocer, Matthew Brembre, became mayor. In dealing with the rich and influential, moreover, the Friar adopts the traditional shopkeeper's servility—"curteis he was and lowely of servyse" (l. 250)—a posture he finds useful wherever "profit sholde arise" (l. 249). In adapting these commercial techniques to the business of begging, the Friar is evidently more successful

---

From *The Chaucer Review* 18, no. 2 (1983).

than the Merchant himself. The Merchant, Chaucer insinuates, may well be in debt; as for the Friar, Chaucer praises him in the technical language of the marketplace which he understands so well: "His purchas was wel bettre than his rente" (l. 256).

These examples are typical of a pattern that informs the General Prologue as a whole. Although not all the pilgrims are as thoroughly enmeshed in the world of commerce as these three, all the pilgrims are described in terms of how they go about getting a living or how they go about spending it, usually on some form of "array." Even the portraits of the unworldly Parson and Plowman are shaped by this essentially commercial outlook. The Parson is described in terms of the customary means for parsons of getting money, sources of income which he himself renounces; he does not hire out his benefice and he does not add to his regular income by working overtime in a chantry. And instead of spending, the Parson gives his money away, both "of his offryng and eek of his substaunce" (l. 489), in other words, both of his income and his capital, as Chaucer notes with a keen eye for the financial niceties. As the Parson gives his money to the poor, so the Plowman gives his labor; he plows for the poor "withouten hire" (l. 538). Likewise, as the Parson gives both of his income and his capital, so the Plowman gives "bothe of his propre swynk and his catel" (l. 540). Although the Parson and the Plowman themselves are evidently removed from the world of commercial values, Chaucer's portraits of them imply an outlook on the part of an audience sufficiently acquainted with the commercial world to recognize the significance of these distinctions between income and capital, and financially sophisticated enough to appreciate the economic dangers of extending the principle of Christian charity so far as to draw down capital in order to give to the poor.

One common explanation of these references to money in the General Prologue is that Chaucer is writing in the tradition of venality satire associated with the literature of the estates. Ruth Nevo, for example, finds the commercial frame of reference "a constant criterion of moral judgement operative throughout the General Prologue." As in venality satire, the references to money, she argues, are designed to call to mind the text which the Pardoner takes as the basis for his sermon and his tale, *radix malorum est cupiditas*. Money in the General Prologue is thus merely a symbol for "cupidity," and, except for the Clerk, the Parson, and the Plowman, Nevo finds all the pilgrims guilty: "Self-indulgent cupidity is the law of their being." This explanation presupposes the audience's awareness of the conventions of venality satire so that they can supply for themselves the references to *cupiditas* and the condemnations of cupidity which are left unstated in the Prologue. One central convention of the genre, however, as Ruth

Mohl has shown in her study of estates satire, is that condemnations of venality are not left unstated, to be supplied by the audience; they are clearly stated and often repeated for rhetorical emphasis, just as Chaucer makes the Pardoner repeat his text, *radix malorum est cupiditas*, twice in the course of his prologue. In an estates satire like the central section of Gower's *Mirour de l'Omme* (ll. 18421–26604), such explicit condemnations of venality recur regularly. If Chaucer is expecting the audience of the General Prologue to read the work as satire and supply such condemnations of venality for themselves, he is violating a basic convention of venality satire itself.

Jill Mann's detailed examination of the relation of the General Prologue to the literature of the estates has called attention to Chaucer's distinctive modifications of that tradition: he departs from the order traditional in estates literature; he omits some traditional figures and adds others which should not, properly speaking, be there; and he adds a wealth of circumstantial detail from the world of work to which each figure belongs, a kind of detail that is not traditionally part of estates literature. Jill Mann's observations provide the background for the hypothesis of this study: in the General Prologue, Chaucer is assuming for both his narrator and his audience a lively interest in the world of getting and spending money, the world of commerce. As narrator, he is neither praising nor condemning that commercial outlook; he is simply taking it for granted. In so doing, Chaucer is making an important departure from attitudes toward the audience traditional both in estates satire and in the kind of courtly literature he knew from his translation of *Le roman de la rose* and experimented with his own love visions. If his assumption of a commercial outlook on the part of his audience for the General Prologue has a literary precedent, it is closest, as Traugott Lawler suggests, to the *fabliaux*. The beginning of the General Prologue, however, has little in common with the beginnings of *fabliaux*, whether French or Chaucer's own; in style and content, the first eighteen lines resemble works like Boccaccio's *Filocolo* or the *Historia Trojana* of Guido delle Colonne, works that assume a courtly or learned outlook on the part of an audience. This same assumption that he is addressing an audience familiar with "courtly" language reappears towards the end of the Prologue, when he apologizes for the plain speech in his descriptions of the pilgrims:

> But first I pray yow, of youre curteisye,
> That ye n'arette it nat my vileynye,
> Thogh that I pleynly speke in this mateere,
> To telle yow hir wordes and hir cheere.
>
> (ll. 725–28)

In introducing commercial references of the sort common in *fabliaux* into a work like the General Prologue, which begins in high style and which is addressed to an implied audience who might accuse an author of "vileynye" or "low" speech if he uses plain language, Chaucer was making a literary experiment of a sort familiar to his modern audience but decidedly unfamiliar to his original audience.

Chaucer's original audience, or his *actual audience*, to use Paul Strohm's helpful terminology, was, I think, "courtly" in the sense in which Richard Green's *Poets and Princepleasers* refines our understanding of the word. But this courtly audience was not removed from the commercial world of fourteenth-century London, as Green and other scholars have made clear. The London ironmonger and moneylender, Gilbert Maghfeld, whose accounts have been printed in part by Edith Rickert, included among his clients not only merchants from more than thirty guilds but also "knights and squires in royal households, several of Chaucer's successors as Controllers in the Customs house, clerks in the Exchequer, many chaplains and parsons, abbots and bishops, the Mayor of London and the Corporation of London as a body, and possibly even the King." Maghfeld certainly enjoyed the King's favor; although he, like the other aldermen of London, was summoned and detained in prison during the quarrel between London and Richard II in 1392, Maghfeld was released sooner than any of the others, restored to his position as alderman, and, in addition, named sheriff. Of all mercantile activities, usury received the harshest official condemnation from the Church, as John T. Noonan, Jr., has documented in detail. Nevertheless, this official condemnation did not, apparently, prevent moneylenders from becoming respected members of the community, and it did not prevent respected members of the community from borrowing or even lending money. Sylvia Thrupp has shown that many of the gentry were engaged, directly or indirectly, in moneylending and commerce, as silent partners, as wholesalers, and as investors; the only apparent restriction seems to have been that a gentleman did not involve himself directly in retail trade. In a manner of speaking, even the King was involved in the wool trade, as Chaucer, the Controller of Customs, was well aware.

Nevertheless, involved as they were in commerce, members of the court and other gentry doubtless did not think of themselves as belonging to the mercantile class, and they did not expect to be addressed as people familiar with the commercial world in a work of polite literature. One of the conventions of courtly literature which Chaucer observes in his other works, for example in the *Troilus*, where he addresses himself to "loveres," is that the *implied audience*, according to Paul Strohm's terminology, is addressed as if they had no interest at all in the commercial world; this supposed indifference to commerce is assumed because people like Chaucer in his capacity as Controller of Customs are preoccupied with "rekenynges," as the Eagle in the *House of Fame* says, and they cannot be expected to know much about the God of Love and his court of lovers.

This conventional separation between the commercial world of getting and spending and the courtly world of love and chivalry informs a central convention of courtly romance. Money may appear in romance, but the commercial activities of buying and selling are rarely mentioned; romance characters may be portrayed as giving or receiving money in the form of largesse or a reward, but they are not shown as involved in the world of commerce and, indeed, the source of their wealth is very seldom specified. Malory's *Gareth*, modeled on romances of the *Bel Inconnu* type, makes this convention the mainspring of the action of the story; Gareth is called "Beaumains" by Sir Kay, who despises him for his desire to earn his keep at Arthur's court by working with his hands in the kitchen.

Fabliaux tend to reinforce this implied separation between commerce and courtliness from the other side. *Fabliau* characters are usually very closely involved in the world of getting and spending, and, in their sexual as well as their other adventures, they repeatedly reveal their ignorance of traditional courtly values. When *fabliau* characters, like Absolon in the Miller's Tale, do attempt to adopt the courtly idiom, they become ridiculous and they usually come to a comic end. This is not the place to review the debate over whether the original audience of the *fabliaux* was courtly or bourgeois, but there is little in the *fabliaux* as a genre that attributes a commercial outlook to the courtly world. "The *fabliaux*," as Charles Muscatine describes them in his review of the question of the social background of the genre, "seem 'lower class,' no matter whose literature they are. No matter what social biases they variously exhibit, they celebrate uniformly one set of values: the ethic of cleverness, of profit, and of elementary pleasure." These values, he notes, are often coupled with language that smacks of the country rather than the city, and they are not simply to be equated with the values associated with an urban and mercantile middle class.

What is new about the General Prologue, and what sets it apart from both the *fabliaux* and the courtly romances, is that the implied audience, whom Chaucer addresses as expert in "curteisye" (l. 725), are addressed as if they were also involved with and interested in the traditional antithesis to the leisured world of the court, the commercial world of money and business. Chaucer assumes that his audience is sufficiently familiar with the courtly world to recognize the faint reflections of that world in the style of the Prioress, Madame Eglentyne. At the same time, he assumes his audience is sufficiently familiar with the commercial world to appreciate the distinction between *purchas* and *rente,* the meaning of a technical term from real estate like *fee simple,* and words from the specialized vocabulary of finance like *bargaynes* and *chevyssaunce.* These words are not used as specialized jargon like the alchemical patter employed by the Canon's Yoeman, but as terms in the common idiom shared by the narrator and the audience. The mixture of courtly and commercial language in the General Prologue evokes in the mind of an audience a mixed world unlike the world of either the romance or the *fabliau,* a world where both a knight and a merchant can be called "worthy," a term of praise traditional of the nobility but, at the same time, a term with its ultimate roots in the world of finance. To put the same point another way, in the General Prologue Chaucer is building into his implied audience an awareness of the commercial realities with which his actual audience was involved. I am not postulating for the *Canterbury Tales* a change from the actual audience addressed in works like the *House of Fame* and *Troilus and Criseyde* or suggesting that the *Canterbury Tales* is a "mercantile epic" in the sense in which Vittore Branca uses the term to describe Boccaccio's *Decameron.* The main point of this study is to suggest that by using commercial language and commercial values in the General Prologue and intermittently throughout the *Canterbury Tales,* Chaucer is making an important innovation in the implied audience he addresses. In an influential article on "Public Poetry in the Reign of Richard II," Anne Middleton defines what she takes to be a central characteristic of Ricardian poetry, "poetry defined by a constant relation of speaker to audience within an ideally conceived worldly community," a community whose essential tone is "high-minded secularism." One of Chaucer's important contributions to public poetry of this sort was his attribution of a shared commercial outlook to both narrator and implied audience in the General Prologue.

A study of the variety of ways in which Chaucer makes use of commercial language and commercial values throughout the *Canterbury Tales* is not possible here. The purpose of this study is simply to suggest that Chaucer's attitude toward these commercial values is complex, and that, as part of that complexity, he devises a rhetorical strategy for the General Prologue which makes the audience a part of the commercial world he is describing. This rhetorical strategy marks an important difference between the Prologue and estates satires, which furnish much of its background. In estates satire, such as the *Vox Clamantis* of John Gower, the author presents himself, and by implication invites the audience to identify with him, as removed from the corrupt world he is attacking; in a visual expression of this stance, Gower portrays himself as an archer, standing somewhere in space and aiming his shafts at the world. In contrast, Chaucer in the General Prologue presents himself as standing on familiar ground, "in Southwerk at the Tabard" (l. 20) he notes, apparently assuming that his audience will recognize the tavern he mentions in this offhand way; at the same time, he assumes a similar familiarity on the part of an audience with the commercial outlook that a tavern represents.

By setting the Prologue in the commercial world of the Tabard, Chaucer is making a radical departure from another convention he observed in his earlier works, a convention that derives ultimately from the *Roman de la rose.* In the *Roman,* the world of the poem, the garden of love which is its subject, is separated from the world of experience by a wall, and the gate through that wall is guarded by *Oiseuse. Oiseuse,* from Latin *otium,* is a word redolent of cultivated leisure, a word opposed to the world of public and commercial activities referred to in Latin as *negotium,* etymologically "absence of leisure." By making *Oiseuse* the gatekeeper to the garden of love, Guillaume de Lorris is embodying in allegorical form the proverbial Ovidian phrase, "Venus otia amat," or "Love loves leisure." Guillaume is also making a statement about the nature of the world of his poem, a world that is entirely removed from the commercial world of *negotium.* By setting his dream vision poems, the *Book of the Duchess,* the *House of Fame,* and the *Parliament of Fowls,* in the privacy of his bedchamber as well as within the most private realm of all, the imaginative world of his dreams, Chaucer is respecting the convention that poetry belongs in the world of *otium.* The *Canterbury Tales,* in sharp contrast, takes its beginning in the very midst of the world of *negotium,* a tavern in Southwark, where Chaucer and his fellow travelers are taking part in a very ordinary business transaction, paying their "rekenynges" for their food and drink (l. 760).

As *Oiseuse* is the gatekeeper to the world of the poetry of *otium* represented by Guillaume de Lorris's *Roman,* so the parallel figure in the world of *negotium* in the *Canterbury Tales* is the innkeeper at the Tabard, Harry Bailly. *Oiseuse,* or *Ydelnesse* in the Middle English *Romaunt,* provides the entrée into the garden of *Deduit,* or *Sir Myrthe* in the Middle English; Harry Bailly, "a myrie man" (l. 757), provides the entrée to the tale-telling game, and he is so intent on interesting the pilgrims in his sort of "myrthe" that he mentions the word three times in his opening speech (ll. 759–68). The implicit contrast between the world of the *Canterbury Tales* and the world of the *Roman de la rose* is reinforced by Chaucer's recurrent references to "ydelnesse." "Ydelnesse" in the *Canterbury Tales* loses the connotations of cultivated ease that belong to *oiseuse* and becomes assimilated to the sin of sloth, the "yate of alle harmes" according to Chaucer's Parson (1.714). Idleness is criticized in similar terms by Dame Prudence in *Melibee,* using words taken from "Salomon": "ydelnesse techeth a man to do manye yveles" ($B^2$2779), or, in the Latin of the ultimate source of the passage, "multum enim malitiam docuit otiositas" (Ecclus. 37:29). Interestingly enough for the argument here, the context of Prudence's use of the biblical injunction against idleness is thoroughly commercial; it appears in the midst of her discussion of "hou ye shul have yow and how ye shul bere yow in gaderynge of richesses, and in what manere ye shul usen hem" ($B^2$2765), that is, in the getting and spending of money. Idleness is at least as great a sin in the commercial world as it is in the religious world of the Parson, as Prudence emphasizes; she cautions Melibee not to be discouraged if there are men more rich and powerful than he, "yet shaltou nat been ydel ne slow to do thy profit, for thou shalt in alle wise flee ydelnesse" ($B^2$2778). The Man of Law, the Clerk, and the Physician also attack idleness in various ways. Even Chaucer's Second Nun denounces idleness, not only in religious terms, as "The ministre and norice unto vices, / . . . That porter of the gate is of delices" (G 1,3), but also in terms familiar to the commercial world of Harry Bailly: "ydelness is roten slogardye, / Of which ther nevere comth no good n'encrees" (G 17–18). *Encrees* is a central concern to the commercial world of *negotium,* a word that brings to mind the Merchant of the Prologue, "Sownynge alwey th'encrees of his wynnyng" (A 275). The Nun's denunciation of idleness in terms familiar to the business world is the more surprising in the mouth of a religious, who is, by her profession, devoted to the religious *otium* of which Father Jean LeClercq has so eloquently written. The *Canterbury Tales* is so pervaded by the commercial outlook that even a sincerely religious nun uses the commercial idiom quite naturally and unselfconsciously.

The most obvious spokesman for the commercial outlook in the *Canterbury Tales* is Harry Bailly, and his repeated reminders of the passage of time throughout the work are another way in which Chaucer evokes the commercial view that time is money and idleness is a waste of time. In fact, the use of Harry Bailly as *fictional audience* in the *Canterbury Tales,* to which Paul Strohm has called our attention, offers some important indications about Chaucer's attitude towards his implied audience as well. Harry Bailly is responsible for the initial plan for the storytelling contest; he proposes it to the pilgrims after they have paid their "rekenynges" for their food and drink at his tavern (a significant detail), as a kind of "play" to occupy their leisure on the trip to Canterbury, and he adds a further incentive, "it shall coste noght" (A 768). What quickly emerges, however, is that Harry's idea of play is in fact part of his characteristic work; someone will pay for the cost of the game and it won't be Harry Bailly. As the judge, Harry will determine the winner in the tale-telling contest, and as innkeeper, he will collect the profits from the winner's meal as well as from the meals of the rest of the pilgrims when they return to the Tabard. Like the Friar, the Summoner, and the Pardoner, Harry knows how to turn a tidy profit from a religious occasion like a pilgrimage.

Harry's keen eye for assessing commercial values emerges clearly in the prologue to the *Canon's Yeoman's Tale* as well. This prologue is set up as a close parallel, almost a parody, of the portraits in the General Prologue, with Harry Bailly asking the questions that lead to the portrait of the newest member of the company. After a few preliminary courtesies, Harry asks the Yeoman about the man with him: "Is he a clerk, or noon? telle what he is" (G 616). By "what he is" Harry obviously means what line of work the man is in, and it is significant that this is the first question he thinks to ask, a question that would be unthinkable in a chivalric romance or a courtly love vision, familiar though it doubtless was in daily life in Chaucer's time as well as our own. The important point is that, in trying to learn who the man is, Harry thinks first of all, not of his name and family connections, nor where he is from, but what he does for a living. When the Yeoman describes his master's skill in the alchemical production of gold and silver, he shows that he understands Harry's meaning perfectly; he does not simply tell him that his master is a canon, which would be a sufficient designation in terms of the tradition of the estates; he also tells Harry, quite literally as it happens, how the man makes money. His answer leaves Harry suspicious. "*Benedicitee!* / This thyng is wonder merveillous to me" (G 628–29), he replies. What astonishes the innkeeper, however, is not the Yeoman's claim that the Canon could pave the entire town of Canterbury with gold and silver, but that a man of the Canon's abilities should appear in public so shabbily dressed:

> His overslope nys nat worth a myte,
> As in effect, to hym, so moot I go!
> It is al baudy and totore also.
> Why is thy lord so sluttissh, I the preye,
> And is of power bettre clooth to beye,
> If that his dede accorde with thy speche?
> (ll. 633–38)

If this Canon is indeed of "so heigh prudence," Harry reasons, why doesn't he dress in such a way as to bring him the "reverence" he deserves? (G 630–32). The underlying logic of this passage is clear: in Harry Bailly's eyes, clothes make the man.

The kind of reasoning Chaucer attributes to Harry Bailly here, making deductions about a man's character and worth on the basis of his patterns of getting and spending money, is typical of the mentality associated with the commercial world that the innkeeper represents. It is also the mentality Chaucer attributes to his implied audience as he goes about describing the pilgrims in the portraits in the General Prologue. Chaucer says that he will tell not only their "degree" but also "whiche they weren" in Harry Bailly's understanding of that question, by describing how they make money. In keeping with the implied interests of his audience, Chaucer also promises to tell about the pilgrims' "array" (A 40), the visible ways in which they spend money on clothes and related appurtenances. Occasionally, Chaucer seems to assume that his implied audience may, like Harry Bailly, draw invidious conclusions from shabby dress; after mentioning that the Knight's *gypon* is "bismotered" (l. 76), he immediately goes on to explain that the Knight had come directly from his battles abroad and that he has with him his son the Squire, who gives by his array a better indication of his father's financial status than does the Knight himself. All these details Chaucer finds necessary, or "acordaunt ot resoun," as he says, in order to enable his audience to assess the "condicioun" of each of the pilgrims (ll. 37–38). *Condicioun* is an especially appropriate word to describe what the portraits in the Prologue convey because it can mean both socioeconomic status and inner character; as Chaucer uses the word in the Prologue it implies an intimate connection between the two.

In describing the pilgrims in this way, Chaucer is attributing to his implied audience a habit of mind they share not only with his fictional audience, Harry Bailly, but with his modern audience as well. All three audiences share the commercial view that what a person does for a living is closely connected with who he is. This assumption is so familiar to Chaucer's modern audience that they may easily overlook what an innovation it represented to his original audience to see themselves in a work of literature as people accustomed to the commercial habit of reading character from economic indicators.

The official destination of the Canterbury pilgrimage is the shrine of Thomas à Becket, but its point of departure is the commercial world of Harry Bailly's tavern. By setting his General Prologue in that commercial world, Chaucer is signaling his departure from literary conventions he observed in his earlier works, including conventions about the implied audience. The extent of his innovation may be appreciated if we remember that a "mercantile epic" like the *Decameron* has a much more conventional setting for its frame: a group of young people with no visible means of support occupy themselves during a period of enforced leisure in a setting very like the garden of love in the *Roman de la rose*; they are playing a tale-telling game, but, despite the commercial content of many of the tales, the game itself has no commercial overtones. Unlike Boccaccio's tales, relatively few of Chaucer's individual tales have a distinctly commercial point of reference, but all his tales are conditioned, directly or indirectly, by the essentially commercial arrangement involved in Harry Bailly's conditions for the tale-telling game, by the continuing presence of Harry as fictional audience and judge of the tales, and by the point of departure and final destination of the group, Harry Bailly's tavern. Equally important, all the tales are also addressed to an implied audience who are assumed to be familiar with the language and outlook of the world of commerce, whatever their social class or source of income. In the General Prologue, Chaucer creates a new kind of implied audience, by implying that his audience will bring a commercial outlook to bear on his text, for the first time in any of his works, and perhaps also for the first time in any work of English literature.

"A Poet Ther Was": Chaucer's Voices in the General Prologue to *The Canterbury Tales*

Barbara Nolan

Chaucer gives us no explicit portrait headed "A Poet ther was" in the General Prologue to *The Canterbury Tales.* Yet the entire Prologue, like so many vernacular invitations to narrative from the twelfth century on, is designed to introduce the poet, describe his task, and gain the goodwill of the audience. Scholars generally agree that the later medieval practice of composing prologues depended on the grammar school study of rhetorical handbooks and classical poetry. By the fourteenth century a self-reflexive prologue conforming to handbook definitions had become more or less de rigueur for aristocratic narrative, both secular and religious. Chaucer's Prologue, though longer and more complex than most, is no exception. It raises expectations in just the areas the handbooks propose, promising to take up important matters of natural and social order, moral character, and religion and outlining the organization the work will follow. Above all, the poet *presents himself,* as the handbooks direct, to ingratiate himself with his listeners or readers and render them receptive to his argument.

Chaucer's Prologue, however, meets these generic expectations in entirely unexpected ways. Most recent critics have recognized that it does not provide a neat, straightforward portrait of the poet. Chaucer's authority remains elusive, exceeding the requirements of the humility topos. Furthermore, whatever potential there may be for coherence in his self-presentation tends to be undermined by the several abrupt changes of style and subject. In fact, the parts of the General Prologue seem to function as

From *PMLA* 101, no. 2 (March 1986). Unless otherwise indicated, translations are by the author.

several attacks on a beginning, each of them probing from a different angle a problem that traditionally belonged to prologues, "How shall I begin and to what purpose?" At first the various styles and subjects juxtaposed in the Prologue appear to suggest no clear answer. Moreover, the parts, or attempts at beginning, are governed not by a single, cumulatively enriched and deepened figure of the poet but, as I argue, by a series of impersonations. None of these taken alone reveals the poet's presence fully. Nor, taken together, do they reveal the poet literary tradition might have led readers to expect.

The General Prologue, I suggest, contains not one voice of the poet but three major attempts at authorical voicing. Each constitutes part of a complex argument about the nature of the poet and poetry in terms authorized by well-known medieval theory and practice. The first of these voices declaims the April opening with the learned assurance and scientific attention of a clerk deliberating in venerable literary formulas on the causes of things. The last is a taven keeper's, urging good cheer and play for material profit. In between we hear the modest, devout "I" of Chaucer the pilgrim, intent on giving systematic order to his experience. But the voices of the other pilgrims so intrude on his own that he is left at last simply with genial apologies for failing to do what he had promised. All the voices are finally Chaucer's, of course, all of them impersonations. And all participate in the poet's complex, unexpected argument concerning his character(s) and purpose.

For the most part, only the voice of the pilgrim has been related to Chaucer's self-presentation. In his well-known and brilliantly persuasive essay, E. Talbot Donaldson urges a separation of the pilgrim from the poet. He argues that the pilgrim persona is a comic device that the poet manipulates as an ironic foil for his own incisive wit. The poet, he says, "operates in a realm which is above and subsumes those in which Chaucer the man and Chaucer the pilgrim have their being."

Few critics have questioned the isolation of the pilgrim persona as Chaucer's principal foil in the Prologue, though several have challenged Donaldson's way of explaining the relationship between the persona and the poet or the man. In an important article and in his book, Donald Howard argues for a more complex and mysterious relationship between the pilgrim and the poet than Donaldson proposes. The pilgrim, he suggests, gives a tantalizingly partial sense of the man behind the work; the limitations invite us to create Chaucer finally in our own image ("Chaucer the Man").

More recently, Marshall Leicester has objected to all interpretations that separate the pilgrim from the poet, contending that the poet's presence is to be discovered not beyond the work but in the voicing of the text. Positing a separation, he argues, gives us the comfortable (and false) sense that we can know who is speaking at any given moment and what position each speaker holds on the matter presented. In his view, it is "just this sense of knowing where we are, with whom we are dealing, that the General Prologue deliberately and calculatedly denies us." Instead of a pilgrim persona juxtaposed with an unimpersonated poet, Leicester proposes the model of a "prologal voice" that belongs to an impersonator preparing to take on the character of each pilgrim in turn. This thesis is provocative, important because it insists that we listen to the text's voicings of character rather than read from preconceived character to text.

But Leicester assumes that such attention to voices should aim at discovering the "personality" of the poet and his pilgrims. This concern for "personality," as also for the presence of the "man," misses the essentially rhetorical, ideologically oriented character of the poet's self-presentation. Heeding Leicester's warning against positing more speakers than necessary and casting Howard's concern for the man in different terms, I argue that Chaucer as a single author projects three major "authorial" voices in his Prologue to examine several possibilities for poetry, all of them empowered by well-known medieval theory and all of them useful for his tales. The three voices lead us not to the poet's "personality" or to Chaucer the man in a general sense but rather to the problem of being a poet in the late fourteenth century. Instead of giving us a single image of the poet and a single definition of the poet's authority, Chaucer juxtaposes images of himself as three possible kinds of poet. The pilgrim is only one of these, though he holds a privileged position among the rest. He is the "I" from whom the others take their being, and he provides a moral center from which to judge the other voices. But an impersonal voice pronounces the opening third-person narration, and Harry's "boold" voice finally replaces the pilgrim's to announce the literary theory and design of the fictive order that follows.

Poetry and poets occupy an uncertain position in medieval theory. Some writers—among them the twelfth-century Platonists, Dante, Petrarch, and Boccaccio—contend that the poet can express truth under the veil of "beautiful lies." In this well-known argument, the reader is to take the fruit, or sentence, and discard the rhetorical chaff of the poet's fictive covering. Another, less generous position—put forward by the Parson in *The Canterbury Tales*—refuses to traffic in "fables" at all. In this view, poetry is frivolity, diversion, false consolation; poets, the perpetrators of falsehood. Chaucer's three voices in the General Prologue form dramatic images of several theories, carrying us from a notion of poetry as philosophy to Harry's view of poetry as distracting merriment.

The argument Chaucer makes about the poet and poetry is neither mechanical nor detached. In the Prologue and in the tales, he explores the whole range of medieval positions regarding poetry, not so much to establish a "true" position as to emphasize his sense of the ambiguities and contradictions surrounding fiction's valuation, and also to turn these difficulties to his advantage. The pilgrim-poet deliberately places himself in the midst of the questions he poses—and he has his pilgrims take up the problem again and again in their prologues and tales. In his many voices, he invites readers to share intimately his quest for a radically new, personal (and ultimately comic, provisional) poetic, one true to his sense of the ironies and limitations inherent in his art of fiction.

I. Multiple Voicing in Medieval Theory and Practice

Multiple voicing as a mode of argument was essential to later medieval narrative, whether in allegorical debate or exemplary private conversation or interior monologue framed by first- or third-person narration. Indeed, romance and allegory, the two dominant narrative forms of the later Middle Ages, positively required multiple voicing. These essentially dialectical forms typically pose challenging social or moral or spiritual questions to be solved by means of the narrative process. Nearly always, the subjectivity of such texts—their grounding in the poet's authority—is presented through two or more voices. Beatrice, Vergil, Raison, Gracedieu, a hermit, a grotesque maiden may serve in the poet's place as a guide to wisdom at various moments in the narrative. By putting on a number of voices, the poet can mask his position and thus draw the audience into an exacting, unpredictable process of discovery.

When we listen to Chaucer's several voices in the General Prologue (and in the tales), therefore, we hear the master of an art cultivated by generations of French and Italian writers. To be sure, in Chaucer the art of playing voice against voice assumes a decisive new direction predictive of the novel's complexities. Yet his invention depended absolutely on the prior discoveries of those major poets who had most influenced him—among them, Benoit de Sainte-Maure, Guillaume de Lorris, Jean de Meung, Boccaccio, Dante, and Machaut.

To find the main theoretical bases for multiple voicing in the Middle Ages, we must turn to the rhetorical handbooks universally used in the grammar schools and to schoolroom exegesis of the curriculum authors.

Handbook discussions give primary attention to calculated voicing and impersonation in the orator's self-presentation and in the acting out of the client's attitudes, feelings, and experiences in order to build a convincing case.

When Quintilian describes the orator's self-presentation in the exordium, or prologue, he recommends an artful management of voice, style, and manner:

> [W]e should . . . give no hint of elaboration in the *exordium*. . . . But to avoid all display of art in itself requires consummate art. . . . The style of the *exordium* . . . should . . . seem simple and unpremeditated, while neither our words nor our looks should promise too much. For a method of pleading which conceals its art . . . will often be best adapted to insinuate its way into the minds of our hearers.
>
> (trans. H. E. Butler)

If artifice and adjustments of voice are to be used even in the defense of honorable cases, they become all the more important for doubtful or discreditable ones.

In this regard, the rhetorical handbooks distinguish between a direct prologue (*principium*) for good causes and a subtle approach (*insinuatio*) for doubtful ones. The *Ad Herennium,* for example, a popular rhetoric attributed to Cicero, defines the difference as follows:

> The direct opening should be such that by . . . straightforward methods . . . we immediately make the hearer well-disposed or attentive or receptive; whereas the Subtle Approach should be such that we effect all these results covertly, through dissimulation, and so can arrive at the same vantage-point in the task of speaking.
>
> (trans. Harry Caplan)

As the classroom handbooks suggest, the assumption of a persona to mask intentions and win favor in the exordium has to do with pragmatic manipulation and strategic dissimulation quite separate from issues of truth and falsehood.

There was also, however, another, larger theory of multiple voicing, propounded in well-known scriptural and literary exegesis. This theory supports the indirect pursuit of true understanding in and through narrative discourse that dramatically represents several opinions, including the author's. Commentators on a variety of texts describe the ways in which a writer can use personae or characters to represent various positions on a given subject. These discussions are rich with suggestion for understanding Chaucer and other vernacular poets. Servius, for example, explaining Vergil's first eclogue, writes:

> A certain shepherd is introduced lying safe and at leisure under a tree in order to make a musical composition; another, indeed, has been expelled from his homelands with his flock, who, when he has seen Tityrus reclining, speaks. And in this place we must understand Vergil under the character [persona] of Tityrus; however, not everywhere, but wherever the argument demands it.

Here, according to Servius, the author presents himself through his characters, not to reveal his personality, but to serve his argument. Tityrus does not always represent Vergil, but speaks for him only when the argument requires it. In this dispensation the author is present not as a distinctive personality but, rather, as a writer strictly speaking, arranging characters and voices in relation to the large argument being made.

In terms still more suggestive for medieval poetry, commentators regularly identify dialogical self-dramatization as a formal feature of some of the most important and influential works of the period, including Augustine's *Soliloquies* and Boethius's *De consolatione.* Of these two texts Peter Abelard says:

> [It is] as if someone, speaking with himself, set up his argument as if two [were speaking], just as Boethius in his book, the *Consolation of Philosophy,* or Augustine in his *Book of Soliloquies.*

And Conrad of Hirsau writes of the *Consolatio:*

> Three characters [personae] are brought forward by Boethius: miserable Boethius seeking to be consoled; Philosophia who consoles; Boethius the author who speaks about both of them.
> (trans. R. B. C. Huygens)

There can be no doubt that such dialogical forms as the *Consolation* and the *Soliloquies,* together with the commentaries surrounding them, provided powerful models for multiple voicing in many kinds of texts throughout the medieval period, but particularly from the twelfth century on.

Gregory the Great's comments on Ecclesiastes offer us yet another full and well-known discussion of the writer's manipulative use of personae and voices in philosophical argument. His description of Solomon's authorial strategies might well have served as a headnote for many a medieval text, including *The Canterbury Tales*. Emphasizing the orator's role in bringing together and reconciling the opinions of a contentious audience, Gregory explains how Solomon impersonates the characters and views of many people as if to pacify a cantankerous crowd:

> This book is called "The Orator" because Solomon takes up there the thinking of a crowd which is in disagreement: under the form of questions he expresses what the man on the street is tempted to think. All the ideas that he takes up in his inquiry correspond to the various characters he impersonates.

According to Gregory, Solomon ends his multivoiced discourse by addressing his listeners in his own voice and drawing them into unity. After he has assumed the many characters and positions leading away from salvation, he argues for the necessity of fearing God and understanding the world's vanity.

Hugh of St. Victor's homily on Ecclesiastes improves on Gregory's description of impersonation and sheds further light on Chaucer's art of multiple voicing:

> [A] many-sided disputation is signified, and [one that has] elicited diverse opinions. For since, in this book, the moral conduct, aspirations, and achievements of many are described, it is necessary for the speaker to assume the voices of many speakers, to express the opinions of many in his discourse, so that he has the power to present the characters of many in his own person, when he who speaks is nonetheless only one. For at the end of the book, having spoken in many [voices], he himself testifies that he has been many [characters] in himself, saying: Let us all equally hear the end of the speaking: "Fear God, and obey his commandments. This is every man." For this is why he wanted to be called "Ecclesiastes" in his work, namely, because his discourse is directed here not to a certain person particularly but to the whole Church—that is, the assembly or multitude of people—and the argument in this book serves at once to portray the conduct of many and to form an image of it.

Of course, Chaucer's art of voicing is far more complex than the kind described by Gregory and Hugh. Among other things it involves a detailed dramatic action so compelling that some eminent critics have assumed that the drama itself was Chaucer's principal concern.

But medieval theorizing about multiple voicing, both the rhetoricians' and the exegetes', suggests a different emphasis, and one well suited to the intricate play of Chaucer's Prologue and tales. While the exegetical comments I have quoted do not explain precisely how multiple voicing works in medieval poetry or in Chaucer, they do provide a rationale for its use and encourage us to examine Chaucer's complex management of voicing with a closer scrutiny than it has generally been given. As I have already suggested, critics propose a false problem when they try to determine who is speaking in a Chaucerian passage—whether, for example, we are to hear the poet or the pilgrim or the man at a particular moment in the General Prologue. The real question is not autobiographical but rhetorical and dialectical. For what rhetorical purpose does the poet assume the pilgrim's voice? How and why is this voice juxtaposed with others in the Prologue and in the tales?

In the General Prologue, we must listen closely to all the voices—the impersonal voice of the opening lines, the pilgrim's, the Host's—as aspects of an argument in which the poet himself participates through his juxtaposition of tonally and stylistically different voices. The poet's presence and his self-definition inhere in his acts of manipulation and his multiple impersonation. Seen in this light, Chaucer emerges from the Prologue, as from the tales, a quick-change artist, a shape shifter, a prestidigitator, a player with voices.

Chaucer's play, however, is more like Solomon's than like Harry Bailly's. It takes the form of an exacting dialectic that dramatically articulates various positions on the human condition. If one attends only to the linear, temporal, narrative process of the Prologue and tales, the play is a source of rich comedy. But for those who assume the poet's perspective as master player and look to the form, the many voices also offer a way to philosophical clarification. By experiencing the voices as parts in a complex argument, the reader, like the poet, may avoid commitment to the misplaced seriousness, the ego attachments, and the foolishness that govern most of the characters. Chaucer's deft juxtapositions of one position with another point in a wise, deep way to the absurdities, the pain, the poignancy, the pretensions, the limited perspectives of the human condition. The poet's own fully conscious play, expressed through his multivoiced dialectic, allows him to acknowledge his fiction making, and that of his characters, for what it is. In this way, he can vindicate the muses of poetry as Boethius could not. Chaucer's play with voices does not issue in a resolution as clear or univocal as Solomon's in Ecclesiastes. Yet the Parson's Tale and the Retraction offer images of finality and closure that *may* bring the Canterbury fictions to an end by an appeal to an order of being beyond the tales.

II. Chaucer's Voices in the General Prologue

As I have suggested, three voices and three attitudes toward poetic authority vie for control in the Prologue—the "clerk's," the pilgrim's, and the Host's. While the first and last are diametrically opposed, the important central voice of the pilgrim mediates between them and explains the unavoidable "fall" from the first to the last in the deliberate absense of a truth-telling allegorical guide. Harry Bailly becomes the necessary muse for *The Canterbury Tales* because no Philosophia or Raison or Gracedieu or Holichurche provides a graceful alternative. But Harry's worldly theory of poetry does not prevail entirely. The other two major prologal voices encourage the possibility of higher poetic aspirations. "Authors" in search of philosophical or spiritual wisdom—like the Knight, the Oxford Clerk, the Second Nun, and the Parson—imitate the clerkly or pilgrim voice in one way or another. In this respect they counter the fictions of others—like the Miller, the Reeve, the Merchant, and the Pardoner—who in one way or another follow the Host in his purely secular play. In addition, the higher voices remain available as alternative models of authority and purpose for readers who will "rewrite" the tales in their private quests for a saving doctrine.

III. The Clerk's Voice

The first of the Chaucerian voices we hear—the first impersonation—gives us the learned poet of the schools. Versed in the literary topoi of the Latin tradition and skilled in rhetorical composition, he is also a scientist of sorts who knows precisely how plants grow and a philosopher who looks into the nature of things.

The rhetorical description of spring spoken in Chaucer's clerkly voice occurs over and over in classical and medieval poets, philosophers, and encyclopedists alike. It belongs to no particular genre or poetic form but appears in a wide variety of contexts—in Lucretius, in Vergil and Boethius, in Carolingian and Goliardic poetry, in encyclopedias like the one by Bartholomeus Anglicus, in scientific manuals like the *Secreta secretorum,* in vernacular lyric and narrative poetry. Whether philosophic or lyrical, the spring topos usually serves as a synecdoche, pointing to the whole order of creation. In medieval lore, spring, as the first of the four seasons, signals the regularity of nature and implies the causal presence of the Creator. In love poetry the arrival of spring may explain the beginnings of erotic feeling and the lover's joyful discovery of his beloved. Or the regularity of spring's appearance may be shown to be at odds with a lover's unseasonal dejection at the loss of his lady.

Like his predecessors, Chaucer in his clerkly guise uses the synecdoche of spring to imply a hierarchy in the universe, one that points inevitably to God as the source of love and order. Within this cosmic scheme Chaucer emphasizes the erotic movement of all creation, imperfect and incomplete, inherently synecdochic, toward completion and the fulfillment of longing. The "when . . . then" construction of the long opening monologue, full of "gret and high sentence," underscores the poet's philosophical urge to explain the causes and laws of things (including human behavior). Within this tight syntactic construction the speaker's facile descent from pilgrimages in general to the Canterbury pilgrimage—from genus to species—exemplifies schoolroom habits of logical thought. Furthermore, the highly literary beginning exactly coincides with its subject, the cosmic beginnings of things, whether in lower nature or in human life. The outer garb of poetry in the high style suits its philosophical subject perfectly, as if the poet could explore and explain the deep matter of natural and human and divine causality.

This sort of beginning sums up a dominant medieval tradition of narrative authority. Just such a voice might well have initiated an allegorical vision of the kind written by Raoul de Houdenc or Dante or Deguileville. Or it might have generated a rewriting of the *Roman de la rose,* exploring the philosophical distinctions between secular and religious love. Allegories like these presuppose the poet's (and humanity's) power to know causes, to give cosmic explications of the kind the first Chaucerian "beginning" seems to promise. The heightened, philosophizing voice is the voice of authoritative literary tradition. It articulates a general longing—shared by poet and readers alike—for a wise, full vision of the human condition and even for entrance into the recesses of divine privity. Yet Chaucer's clerkly articulation of the poet's task is abruptly truncated. It remains a fragment, a possibility unexploited. In the very next section of the Prologue a second voice definitively denies access to the high mysterious realm of causes—a realm that had been confidently explored by medieval poets of the greatest importance, including Bernard Silvestris, Alain de Lille, and Dante.

IV. The Pilgrim's Voice

The poet's startling shift from a clerk's voice to a pilgrim's turns on the important world *bifil.* It is a word that, together with *bifalle, falle,* and *fil* in the same sense, occurs often in the course of *The Canterbury Tales.* It typically signifies chance happenings, unexpected events occurring at random. The order of time governed by *bifil* and *fil* is radically different from the mythic, cyclic time of the spring topos. It is, in fact, the "order" of the fallen historical world, in which chance, change, unpredictability hold sway. Nor is this time synecdochic; unlike the springtime imagery, it does not point beyond itself. By its nature it does not lend itself to allegory and the wise explication of causes but, rather, supports the more modest claims of chronicle, storytelling, and confession.

The abrupt break in Chaucer's introductory monologue, initiated by the world *bifil* and dominated by a personal "I," constitutes just the sort of "semantic reversal" that the Czech critic Jan Mukarovsky has singled out as a sign of "dialogic discourse" (*The Word and Verbal Art*). We are unexpectedly jolted from the monologic structure of the clerkly discourse, largely free of involvement in specific time or space, to the pilgrim's direct dialogic address to the other pilgrims and to the readers. Mukarovsky's description of this kind of discourse precisely suits the complex interplay in the pilgrim's speech as the "I" introduces himself and the other pilgrims: "by a sleight of hand the listener becomes the speaker, and the function of the carrier of the utterance constantly jumps from participant to participant."

We observe immediately that the character into which the poet has "fallen" defines him as essentially imperfect, incomplete, on the way: "I lay / Redy to wenden on my pilgrymage / To Caunterbury with ful devout corage" (1.20–22; F. N. Robinson, 2d ed.). Through his pilgrim "I" as the central voice in the Prologue, Chaucer exploits to the full the humility topos the rhetorical handbooks recommend for the exordium. He genially claims incompetence in the art of making arguments, and he speaks directly and personally to his audience with the same ingratiating deference he had evidently used in insinuating himself into the fellowship of pilgrims. As we follow Chaucer's development of the pilgrim's character, however, we discover that the device is no mere device. The pilgrim persona is not just a mask but a central fact of this and every poet's existence. Chaucer's genius here, as elsewhere, lies in his ability to transform a familiar topos into a precise metaphor.

The image of the pilgrim is heavy with meaning, though critics have had a tendency to pass lightly over it, settling for its function as a comically ironic front for the poet. In fact, this assumption leaves us with an incomplete understanding of Chaucer's point in having his central persona and voice develop as they do. Chaucer gives us not a poet assuming the guise of a pilgrim but a pilgrim attempting the poet's task. His "I" persona identifies the speaker as *first* a pilgrim. The priority thus defined is an important one because it establishes an ontological perspective from which to measure all the rhetorical play recorded in the portraits.

How are we to interpret this voice, this image, if we take it seriously as a necessary replacement for the clerkly voice? As pilgrim, the poet participates in "corrumpable" nature, acknowledging by his pilgrimage that his nature takes its beginning from a being greater than himself and finds its end beyond himself in a "thyng that parfit is and stable" (1.3009). The pilgrim, like Everyman, proceeds at least to some extent "dronke . . . as is a mous" who "noot which the righte wey is thider" (1.1261, 1263). Of course the pilgrim Chaucer is not the lovesick Arcite or the drunken Miller of any of the other "sondry folk" in and out of the tales. but he claims fellowship with them. His identity and his voice are intimately bound up with theirs, and he discovers his own powers and limits by investigating theirs.

The pilgrim insists that his investigation be made not from the superior vantage point assumed by the clerkly voice but from within: "I was of hir felaweshipe anon, / And made forwarderly for to ryse, / To take *oure* wey ther as I yow devyse" (1.32–34). Chaucer the pilgrim submits himself explicitly to the demands and limits of the occasion "in *that* seson on *a* day" (l. 19). And he makes an immediate accord with the motley crowd of travelers who have come together at the Tabard "by aventure" (l. 25). Accepting their chance fellowship as a matter of course, he assumes the responsibility of telling us about them and their plans. Instead of casting about in old books and authorities for material, as his clerkly and courtly predecessors had typically done, Chaucer simply "finds" the matter that has fallen in his way—the flesh and blood (and words) of his fellows at the Tabard. Instead of remaining apart from this matter to infuse it with wise meaning, the pilgrim joins the group, becomes a part of the matter he proposes to investigate and invest with form.

Now from the point of view of literary history such involvement is not unprecedented. Dante had, after all, admitted his own participation in the sins of his purgatorial ascent—particularly lust and pride. Yet he had also styled himself a visionary, blessed with a higher understanding of his matter, able to transcend his mortal blindness by intellect and grace. Chaucer the pilgrim, by contrast, eschews the perspective of the allegorist and the comforts of enlightenment. The relationship he establishes with his pilgrim characters and their stories is rather the historian's than the visionary's.

Indeed, in his self-defining art of portraiture in the General Prologue and in the imitation he proposes to undertake, the pilgrim as *auctor* probably owes his greatest debt to the literary example of Dares, the self-styled eyewitness chronicler of the Trojan War. Dares, perhaps chiefly through his medieval "translators," had profoundly influenced Chaucer in writing the *Troilus*. In the General Prologue, the influence of Dares and his progeny appears once again, this time as part of the poet's complex defense of his art. Chaucer the pilgrim, like Dares, claims direct, personal observation as the basis for his "true" writing. But in the Prologue, the historian's voice is absorbed into the character of the pilgrim-poet and linked to a game of storytelling.

The connection Chaucer makes in linking the pilgrim persona, historiographic mimesis, and the Canterbury fictions is deep and important, for it crystallizes one of the most painful lessons of medieval Christianity: that human beings in their condition of exile must depend for their knowledge on limited powers of observation, an imperfect understanding of events, and a language essentially different from, and inadequate to, the truths it seeks to express.

The pilgrim-poet acknowledges his metaphysical condition most directly at the end of his "historiographic" portrait gallery in the well-known declaration "My wit is short, ye may wel understonde" (1.746). This disclaimer is most often interpreted as a tongue-in-cheek gesture, the calcualted stance of a brilliant bourgeois before his social betters. And it probably is an opportune rhetorical strategy. But, as is often true in Chaucer, the surface significance may be shown to belie a deeper, or even opposite, sense. If we consider the apology not only a ploy but also a straightforward, nonironic statement of fact—and the language, as well as medieval theology, allows us to do so—then Chaucer's self-definition as poet assumes a new direction in this central voice. The pilgrim seeks to authorize himself not by his brilliance or learning or moral perspicuity but by his common humanity. If we read *wit* in its central medieval acceptation as "power of knowing and understanding" rather than as "ingenuity" only, the clause "My wit is short" assumes a philosophical sense. Absolute shortness of wit supplies a principle of organization whereby the poet may bypass high cultural literary order in favor of a larger, ironic inquiry into the sorry but also comic plight of the human spirit in this world's exile.

V. The Pilgrim's Portrait Gallery

In every aspect of his self-presentation, Chaucer's pilgrim persona practices a comically incomplete power of "devysyng," one that reveals the *humana fragilitas* in the historian's stance. He begins his portrait series with the confident formula "A Knyght ther was" (1.43), as if he intends to uncover the nature of each social type by giving a full, precise, ordered example. The formula proposes rhetorical and philosophical plenitude by way of synecdoche; yet the text fails to deliver fullness or completeness. Individual characters systematically escape from or evade the expected formulas, leaving us with a sense not only of the social "obsolescence" Donald Howard has suggested but also of an essential partiality and eccentricity (*Idea*).

Through his voice as pilgrim-historian, Chaucer structures the portraits so as to deny us a clear, total representation of the individuals as types related to transcendent ideals. The portraits fail to arrange themselves in a recognizable hierarchical order, an order that would call our attention to the expected, or "proper," order of society. Nor, for the most part, do the eccentric characters who claim nominal participation in the various estates fully clarify their preordained roles, either negatively or positively. The ideal knight, the ideal monk and friar, the ideal wife (or their systematically developed opposites) remain notions partly beyond the horizon of the text.

What is important in the fictions of the portrait gallery is that the pilgrim participates in them, allowing his "exemplary" figures to overtake his own voice dialogically through indirect discourse. As rhetor and historian, Chaucer delights in his pilgrims as dramatis personae. He observes, often with admiration, the details of their self-dramatization—the fictions they project to fool themselves or to impress, cajole, or exploit others.

Yet, if the pilgrim-poet were *homo rhetoricus* and secular historian only, there would be no moral center against which to measure the wanderings and eccentricities of those he describes. And the portraits would lack just the tension that gives them their lasting power and point. In fact, the amorality of the historian's rhetorical stance is pervasively countered by reminders of a nonrhetorical, suprahistorical mode of existence. Not only the "ful devout corage" of the pilgrim himself but also the figure of the Parson provides a point of reference for this alternative mode. The Parson's "pose"—or, more properly, "role"—as a shepherd conscientiously caring for his flock approximates his central identity. He imitates Christ the Good Shepherd in every detail of his life and thereby identifies himself exclusively as a son of God. Indeed, our *only* image of the Parson's physical presence is that of a Christian shepherd of souls with staff in hand. What Chaucer emphasizes in the Parson's portrait is the coincidence of word and deed, of Christian teaching and high moral conduct. There is in the Parson's life little matter for "troping," little rhetorical distance between his soul's self and his outward presentation.

From the perspective of Christian pilgrimage, the social or religious roles of most of the other characters appear to be added onto them, like their costumes, often accompanied by distorting or falsifying elaborations. The Knight's remarkable achievements in battle, the Pardoner's fashionable cape, the Friar's girlfriends, the Wife of Bath's old and young husbands—all distract the pilgrims more or less from their single proper concern, the destiny of their souls. In rhetorical terms, the lives and speech of most of the pilgrims are "troped," turned in one way or another away from transcendent truth in the direction of Harry Bailly's kind of worldly fiction making.

Both the Parson's life and the poet's brilliant juxtapositions of detail call attention to the artifices the pilgrims practice. The obvious contradictions between pretension and fact encourage us to recognize the fictions for what they are. Yet we do not hear in the pilgrim's portraits the voice of the strict moralist anatomizing human folly with clerical rigor. In his rendering, the fictions of daily life in the temporal world of "bifil" coincide with the fictions of art, and the poet exploits, even as he delights in, the coincidence.

For an anagogically "true" reading of the poem's matter we must wait for the Parson. It is he who will insist on a definitive separation of fact and truth from fiction:

> Thou getest fable noon ytoold for me;
> For Paul, that writeth unto Thymothee,
> Repreveth hem that weyven soothfastnesse,
> And tellen fables and swich wrecchednesse.
>
> (10.31–34)

Chaucer might have given the Parson's voice to himself as "I" from the beginning. Had he done so, however, he would have had to reject all the "pley," all the voices, of *The Canterbury Tales*. Boethius's Lady Philosophy, it will be remembered, had rejected the muses of falsifying, consolatory poetry at the start of his *Consolation*. In pointed (and I think calculated) contrast, Chaucer's Retraction comes only at the end of his work. The very existence of the tales depends on his deliberately *not* beginning as Boethius had, not rejecting the sweet venom of fiction until its pleasures and possibilities have been fully explored as well as exposed.

VI. The Pilgrim Voice and the Question of Truth

The pilgrim broaches the question of truth, and broaches it explicitly, in the General Prologue. Yet when he invokes a Platonic theory to support his tale-telling, he misapplies the theory and thereby brilliantly defers the question of a transcendent truth beyond the truth of historical reportage:

> Whoso shal telle a tale after a man,
> He moot reherce as ny as evere he kan
> Everich a word, if it be in his charge,
> Al speke he never so rudeliche and large,
> Or ellis he moot telle his tale untrewe,
> Or feyne thyng, or fynde wordes newe.
> . . . .
> Eek Plato seith, whoso that kan hym rede,
> The wordes moote be cosyn to the dede.
> (1.731–36; 741–42)

Here, in a flagrant misreading, the pilgrim comically conflates his own "historiographic" notion of truth as the imitation of passing life with Plato's theory relating words to the transcendent truth of things. We may pass lightly over the conflation and assume that the poet is simply pleading for a new kind of artistic freedom. But Chaucer seems to intend something deeper by deliberately juxtaposing the pilgrim's and Plato's ideas of imitation. In placing his theory cheek by jowl with Plato's, he aims, I think, to provide a mortal correction for what he considers an impossible dream.

The pilgrim's description of his language is straightforwardly *anti*allegorical in an age that generally revered allegorical poetry: his words will not, at least easily or directly, point to things (or truth or doctrine) as words were said to do in allegorical poems like the *Roman de la rose.* They will simply imitate the words and "chiere" of the other pilgrims, which are neither Platonic "things" nor stable ideas, but transient phenomena. The text as a collection of unstable, ambiguous signs will mark the beginning rather than the completion of speculation about the nature of things. The poet in his pilgrim voice will not be a philosopher or a repository of high wisdom, at least not in a traditional sense. Instead he will simply be an earthly maker and historian, putting idiosyncratic words and actions together according to his limited powers of observation and invention and the unpredictable demands of the matter. Chaucer the pilgrim, like Dares the historian, thus turns the text over to the audience, who will have to interpret or translate the signs into meaning, discerning the "true" inner structure informing the ensemble of outward manifestations. While this management of the poet's and the audience's roles may appear modern, or even postmodern, it is in fact thoroughly explicable as a logical (though also brilliantly original) development from dominant medieval theories concerning fiction and the limits of human knowledge.

The Platonic theory Chaucer's pilgrim invokes originated in the *Timaeus,* and versions of it appear in many a medieval text, including Boethius's *Consolation* and Jean de Meung's *Roman de la rose.* Underlying all the arguments from Plato to Jean is a confidence that words describe objective, knowable, nameable reality, whether that reality is the motions of the will (Plato) or ideas in the mind (Chalcidius) or God (Boethius) or testicles (Jean de Meung). For writers of fictions, the theory provided some assurance that poetic narratives—"beautiful lies" according to the dominant learned tradition—could legitimately explore the causes of things and teach truth. In Boethius and Jean, voices of authority—Philosophia, Raison, the Poet—speak the theory. Their authority is in a certain sense absolute. They grant the poet and therefore the reader power to cut through the artifices of allegorical fabrication to touch the secrets of philosophy.

What distinguishes Chaucer from earlier poets is that he refuses to give the Platonic doctrine to an authority figure. Instead of speaking it through Philosophia or Raison or Gracedieu, he presents it through his pilgrim voice. The pilgrim as historian proposes to use words not to represent things or truth or doctrine or ideas, as a clerk would have done, but to mimic the transient words and gestures of others. These acts belong to the sundry folk of the fallen world, who are not likely, by and large, to speak or behave philosophically. Some of them are counterfeiters. Some are professional (lying) rhetoricians. Others are professional cheaters or tricksters or swindlers. Of course all of them are finally given voice by Chaucer. All are part of his grand masquerade, and all represent aspects of his self-presentation as pilgrim-poet.

Paradoxically, the pilgrim's very act of mimicry bespeaks an oblique recognition of the truth about his poetry. On one side of his equation are the stories he and his subjects offer—the fictions they construct about themselves as well as those they construct for the game's sake. On the other is his own *humana fragilitas,* yearning for, needing transcendent truth, the explanation of causes, but bound by the necessities of limited wit, imperfect observation, ambiguous language, and inevitable mortality. The pilgrim-poet can do no more than endeavor to record and illustrate these limitations, using trope and omission at every turn to acknowledge his distance from truth and wholeness. As a sort of magician, an illusion maker, he—like the Orleans clerk of the Franklin's Tale, or the Fiend of the Friar's Tale—can only make free with necessities. His tellers, in presenting themselves as "characters" and telling their tales, will propose causal explanations for themselves and try to elucidate the events of their stories. But the explanations will be limited finally by their fictiveness. Only the Parson's Tale will probe the true causes of things directly, but his "tale" is not a fiction. The language of the tales is deliberately and designedly the language of error, as judged by an unrealized, extratextual language of transcendent truth.

In the pilgrim's argument, fiction, like history, is a necessity imposed by the Fall. Chaucer's pilgrim voice as it mingles with the voices of the other Canterbury pilgrims proclaims the delights of tale-telling. The poet willingly, even willfully, engages the fallen world's illusions, opinions, and beliefs, questioning by his play their relations to truth.

Is there, then, any "truth" to be found in the pilgrim's report of the Canterbury adventure? And, if so, where and how? As the orchestrator of all the artifices, all the falsifications, all the voices of the *Tales,* the pilgrim Chaucer unashamedly encourages his fictive surrogates in their mendacious enterprises. A shapeshifter and a trickster, he himself thrives on lying. Yet because he styles himself a pilgrim, his lying, like that of the Fiend of the Friar's Tale, may be read as part of God's service. The Fiend, as he tells the summoner, lies partly because human "wit is al to bare" to understand the truth (3.1480). Even when he tells the summoner the transcendent truth about himself—recessed within the fiction of his bailiff disguise and voice—the summoner fails to grasp it. In a parallel way, Chaucer gives his tellers matters of truth in their stories, but the truth more often than not remains unobserved by the tellers and their characters within the fictive frames.

Of course, as the Fiend says, some withstand "oure temptacioun"—see through the disguises—and this act is "cause of [their] savacioun" (3.1497–98). Multiple (and wrong) interpretation must be the rule in reading the "divers art and . . . diverse figures" of the Fiend and the pilgrim-poet alike (3.1486). Yet Chaucer, like the Fiend, holds out the possibility of "right" interpretation. Such interpretation, however, will depend more on the reader's intention than on the fiction itself—the individual's personal concern for truth and salvation.

Chaucer provides this saving extraliterary definition of fiction and interpretation not through his pilgrim but through his final voice and final image in *The Canterbury Tales*. In his retraction after the Parson's Tale, he says, " 'Al that is writen is writen for oure doctrine,' and that is myn entente" (10.1083). The poet is this last voice also begs pardon for any of his tales that "sownen into synne" and apologizes for his "enditynges of worldly vanitees" (10.1085, 1084). Yet, while he, like the Fiend, warns of the dangers of fiction, he knows that his audience may not heed the warning. In fact, he himself has succumbed to temptation in allowing his many fictive voices to enjoy the delights of Harry's game.

VII. The Host's Voice

Harry Bailly's voice, which dominates the final movement of the General Prologue, follows directly from the pilgrim's declaration "My wit is short." From that point on, another "I," another character, empowered by the pilgrim voice, assumes control over the design of the tales. Like most Chaucerian transitions, the juxtaposition of the apologetic voice with Harry's portrait and his "boold" speech requires more than cursory attention. It is as if Harry were born of the pilgrim-poet's essential limitation.

Yet, as a child of insufficiency, Harry lacks the self-critical awareness of his parent. Like the pilgrim, he espouses a theory of fiction. But while his notion of "making"—the third in Chaucer's series in the General Prologue—coincides with the pilgrim's in fundamental ways, it lacks the pilgrim's acknowledgment of partiality, limitation, and absence. Despite Harry's pious bow to "sentence" in the General Prologue, his fiction is essentially fiction for the sake of play and mirth and also for financial profit. As such, it is a fiction unmoored in ideas about truth or the quest for truth.

Harry, the fourteenth-century bourgeois innkeeper, has often been regarded as an "original," having no clear literary antecedents. Manly even identifies him with a historical Henry Bailly, thus establishing his credentials as a "realistic" character. Like so many other Chaucerian characters, however, Harry owes his originality not only to his apparently idiosyncratic, realistic "condicioun" and "chiere" but also to the poet's complex manipulation of well-established literary and theoretical formulations. Understood as the latter-day spokesman for an ancient tradition, Harry assumes a climactic place in Chaucer's dialectical argument concerning the character of the poet and the functions of poetry.

We first meet Harry Bailly in the dining room of his inn after he has served supper to his guests and collected their bills. For this third major voice in Chaucer's complex introductory defense of his fiction, the context has narrowed significantly. The vast panorama of the external, seasonal world served as locus for the clerkly voice. An entire inn treated *as* an inn—a place on the way—framed the pilgrim. By contrast, a single public room designed for drinking and eating encloses Harry's authority and poetic theory. And Harry is at home in the Tabard. As the scene narrows, so too do the possibilities for poetry as an art of wise interpretation. In the dining room of a tavern we listen to the host's limited and limiting notions about the poet and poetry.

As the innkeeper "reads" poetry, it fully deserves the notoriety assigned to it by the stricter antique and medieval theorists, from Paul, Augustine, and Boethius to Chaucer's Parson. Harry sponsors fiction for reasons very like those of Boethius's muses—the "scaenicas meretriculas" "theatrical whores"—at the beginning of the *Consolation*. The Muses that Lady Philosophy dismisses from Boethius's chamber are those Plato and Cicero had also condemned, those who inspire laments over bad fortune and celebrate pleasure as the proper goal of poetry (and life). Some medieval commentators widened Philosophia's condemnation to include all secular poetry. As one exegete puts it, Boethius's "theatrical whores" are the "Musas quas inuocant illi qui saeculariter scribunt Horatius Virgilius et alii qui nouem Musas nouem deas fingunt et inuocant" "The Muses whom those invoke who write in a wordly way: Horace, Vergil, and others who depict the nine Muses as nine goddesses and invoke them" (trans. Edmund T. Silk). In the environment of philosophy, so the medieval commentator's argument goes, all worldly poetry is to be recognized as falsifying fiction. Later theorists—among them Petrarch and Boccaccio—fully aware of such religiously based opposition to secular poetry, took pains to redress the criticisms. They insisted with humanist zeal on the correctness of ancient definitions that allow poetry both its fictive covering and its truth. Chaucer, by contrast, turns over the direction of his poetry making to Harry Bailly and thereby gives a hearing to a notion of poetic fiction divorced from the philosophical search for truth.

Despite his brief, perfunctory bow to Horatian "sentence," Harry prefers poetry as mirthful distraction from the hard realities and pain of the human condition. His interest in tale-telling coincides with his pleasure in drinking and, covertly, his desire for money. This last use of fiction for profit aligns him particularly with Boethius's theatrical strumpets. As Nicholas Trivet puts it in his commentary on the *Consolation,* "the poetic muses are called theatrical whores—[because] just as a whore copulates with those [lovers] for love not of procreation but of lucre, so poets were writing about those [things]—for the love not of wisdom but of praise, that is to say, of money." Harry's ultimate goal in generating the fictions of the Canterbury journey is to collect the price of twenty-nine suppers, minus his own small contribution to the winner's meal at the end of the trip.

As a master of mirth, Harry is also kin to the all-important figure of Déduit in Guillaume de Lorris's *Roman de la rose*. This character, whom Chaucer called "Sir Mirth" in his translation of the *Roman,* is the courtly proprietor of the garden into which the poet enters as a young lover (about to be trapped by erotic desire). In this garden Déduit acts as choragus for a troop of jongleurs, jugglers, musicians, singers, and dancers. In a parallel way, Harry in his dining room proposes himself as the leader of a band of fiction makers. As Déduit's followers are distracted by the garden's "siren" birds and the music of his players, Harry's pilgrims succumb without demur to the innkeeper's strong wine and promises of mirth through storytelling.

Above all, both Déduit and Harry traffic in "divertissement." In Chaucer's translation of the *Roman,* Sir Mirth in the garden "walketh to solace . . . for sweeter place / to pleyen ynne he may not find" (ll.621–23). Like Guillaume's allegorical figure, Harry, who seeks play for the sake of solace, is essentially mirthful. The words *mirth, myrie, pley, disport,* and *comfort* appear twelve times in twenty-six lines as Chaucer gives us Harry's portrait and has him explain his game. The very name Déduit suits both characters exactly, containing as it does the two senses "having a good time" and "turning away from a [right] course" (trans. Charles Dahlberg). To be sure, Harry and his followers leave the Tabard and walk out into the world engaged to play a diversionary game, whereas Déduit remains at home in his symbolic garden. Yet Harry sees to it that his pilgrim subjects never forget that they have contracted to remain within the bounds of his play and his notions of solace. The fictions themselves, together with Harry's framing commentary, become the pilgrims' "pleasure garden" for the duration of the Canterbury journey. At the same time, however, the inescapable fact of the pilgrimage serves as an ever-present critique of the game, reminding us that there is another, "right" course.

While Harry, in framing his game, shares Déduit's concern for mirth and solace, his image of diversionary art is richer and more philosophically complex than his French counterpart's. In his avowed antipathy of silence and his intended use of fiction for financial profit, he sums up Boethius's whole argument concerning the conflict between distracting fictions and the search for philosophical truth. Harry's kind of fiction explicitly opposes the silence of spiritual introspection proper to the life of true pilgrimage. Poetry is, for him, a pleasant noise that keeps the mind conveniently distracted from any pilgrim sense of the need for truth or meditation on the *lacrimae rerum.* "And wel I woot," he says,

> as ye goon by the weye,
> Ye shapen yow to talen and to pleye;
> For trewely, confort ne myrthe in noon
> To ride by the weye doumb as a stoon;

And therfore wol I maken yow disport,
As I seyde erst, and doon yow som confort.
(1.771–76)

Harry's interest in distraction coincides with his pervasive urge to rush from one tale to another. Gaps in diversionary discourse, like the absence of mirth, may allow introspection to enter, and this Harry cannot bear.

Why, we must ask, does Chaucer turn over the important last place in his prologal argument to so disreputable a voice and position? He does so at least in part, I believe, to give a full, unabridged account of all aspects of the fiction he proposes to write. Like Dante in the *Commedia,* he intends to include—and even praise—the impure, infernal element in his poetry as well as its potential for philosophical vision. Indeed, poetry as rhetorical bedazzlement may have seemed to him the most evident, accessible, attractive aspect of his art, the one most likely to charm his audience into paying attention. By way of Harry's voice, Chaucer, unlike many of his critics, defends (though with the substantial reservations imposed by the other prologal voices) the delights of puzzlement, diversion, and absorption in the illusions wrought by rhetorical coloring.

Through Harry, Chaucer also calls attention to the common tendency, in which the tavern keeper's notion of fiction making participates, to miss or set aside contemplation of the providential design of the universe and humanity's place within it. Storytelling, at least at one level, affords a pleasure not unlike the Wife's putative joy in wealthy and virile husbands, the Friar's enjoyment of rich patrons and comfortable taverns, the Monk's pleasure in hunting, January's delight in his love garden, and the myriad other diversions by which the Canterbury characters live. Chaucer the poet does not exempt himself or his writing from this pleasurable, spiritually subversive function of fiction. But he admits his involvement in so disreputable a cause only indirectly, as a good orator should, using Harry's voice and character to mask his own. In his last voice, Chaucer slyly celebrates poetry in just the terms that the strictest theorists had used to condemn it.

In doing so, however, Chaucer is not giving Harry's ideas about poetry precedence over other, higher notions. Like the opening formulations of the clerkly voice, the Host's game provides a framing contrast for the central, dynamic notion of the poetic enterprise in the General Prologue—the one articulated by the pilgrim's voice. The voices of the clerk and the innkeeper offer relatively fixed, static images of poetry: one is concerned with causality, hierarchy, and order, the other with the disorders, sexual exploits, and trivialities of quotidian life. Both positions are curiously abstracted, though in opposite ways, from the complex central subject of poetry as the pilgrim voice proposes it—human consciousness of a universe that emanates from God but also participates in entropy, mortality, disintegration.

Neither the first nor the last notion of poetry entertained in the General Prologue allows for the rich, active, tentative, dialogic exploration of that difficult subject as the pilgrim voice engages it. The pilgrim Chaucer may reach upward toward the clerk's philosophical formulations or downward to Harry's bourgeois laughter. He is bound by neither, though he may play with both. His deeply human engagement with his flawed, mortal subject and art precludes direct statements of transcendent truth in his fiction. By the same token, his storytelling will rise above the category of fictions made simply for the sake of rhetorical play and distracting frivolity. What remains—the poetry at the center—is fictive, certainly. But it is as richly various and morally dense and stubbornly inconclusive as its total subject. Its selfconscious fictionality will press well-disposed readers toward a new awareness of the nature of illusion and self-deception, whether in literature or in life. The truths the tales uncover have to do mainly with human ways of knowing (and not knowing) the self and the mortal world.

To find the truths of Christian doctrine, however, one must set the tales aside. Transcendent truth remains largely absent from the Chaucerian narratives, and it must. In Chaucer's argument, this is just the kind of truth that makes all secular fiction untenable. Nonetheless, Chaucer the poet in his several voices points directions, marks boundaries, poses questions and puzzles that bear heavily on the truths beyond his fictions.

Chronology

ca. 1340–45	Geoffrey Chaucer born, probably in the wine-marketing area of London, Vintry Ward. His parents, Agnes and John Chaucer, are wealthy property owners; John is a prosperous London wine merchant.
1357	Chaucer serves as a page to Elizabeth de Burgh, Countess of Ulster.
1359–60	Chaucer serves in King Edward III's army in France. He is captured, but Edward pays his ransom.
ca. 1366	Chaucer marries Philippa Roet. He begins his association with John of Gaunt, probably through his wife, whose sister, Katherine Swynford, is John of Gaunt's mistress. John Chaucer dies.
1367	As a member of King Edward III's household, Chaucer receives a royal annuity.
ca. 1368–71	Writes *The Book of the Duchess.*
ca. 1372–80	Writes *Saint Cecilia,* which later becomes the Second Nun's Tale, and some of the Monk's tragedies.
1372–73	Sent to Genoa and Florence in the service of the King, Chaucer probably becomes acquainted with the writings of Boccaccio, Petrarch, and Dante. He may also have met Petrarch.
1374	Chaucer moves to the house over the gate of Aldgate. Edward III appoints him Controller of the Customs and Subsidies on Wool for the port of London.
1377	Chaucer travels to France on the King's behalf. While he is there, Edward III dies and Richard II becomes king. Richard renews Chaucer's customs appointment and confirms his royal annuity.

1378	Richard II sends Chaucer to Milan, where he renews his acquaintance with Italian literature.
ca. 1378–80	Writes *The House of Fame.*
1380	Cecilia Chaumpaigne sues Chaucer for *raptus*. He is cleared of all responsibility.
ca. 1380–82	Writes *The Parliament of Fowls.*
1382–85	Chaucer is appointed Controller of the Petty Customs, but then begins to phase himself out of his customs jobs by appointing full-time deputies.
ca. 1382–87	Chaucer translates Boethius's *Consolation of Philosophy* and writes *Troilus and Criseyde, Palamoun and Arcite* (the Knight's Tale), *The Legend of Good Women,* and other shorter works.
1385	Appointed Justice of the Peace for Kent.
1386	Chaucer is elected to Parliament as one of the two "Knights of the Shire" to represent Kent. He gives up his house at Aldgate and his controllerships.
1387	Philippa Chaucer dies. Chaucer loses his royal annuity and goes into debt. He travels to Calais.
ca. 1387–92	Writes the General Prologue and the earlier of the *Canterbury Tales.*
1389	Richard II appoints Chaucer Clerk of the King's Works.
ca. 1390–91	Chaucer oversees construction and repair on several buildings, including the Tower of London, Westminster Palace, and St. George's Chapel at Windsor Castle. Usually carrying substantial amounts of money, he is robbed several times and possibly is injured.
1391	Chaucer relinquishes his clerkship and is appointed deputy forester of the Royal Forest at North Petherton in Somerset.
ca. 1391–93	Writes *A Treatise on the Astrolabe.*
ca. 1392–95	Writes most of the *Canterbury Tales* during this period.
1394	Richard II grants Chaucer a new royal annuity.
ca. 1396–1400	Chaucer writes the latest of the *Tales,* including probably the Nun's Priest's Tale and the Canon's Yeoman's Tale, and several other shorter poems.
1399	John of Gaunt dies. Later in the year, Richard II is deposed and killed; Henry IV becomes king. Henry confirms Chaucer's pension and grants him an addi-

tional annuity. Chaucer leases a house in the garden of Westminster Abbey.

1400 Chaucer dies, probably sometime between June and October, and is buried in Westminster Abbey.

Contributors

HAROLD BLOOM, Sterling Professor of the Humanities at Yale University, is the author of *The Anxiety of Influence, Poetry and Repression,* and many other volumes of literary criticism. His forthcoming study, *Freud: Transference and Authority,* attempts a full-scale reading of all of Freud's major writings. A MacArthur Prize Fellow, he is general editor of five series of literary criticism published by Chelsea House. During 1987–88, he served as Charles Eliot Norton Professor of Poetry at Harvard University.

RUTH NEVO is Professor of English at Hebrew University at Jerusalem. She is the author of *The Dial of Virtue: A Study of Poems on Affairs of State in the Seventeenth Century, Comic Transformations in Shakespeare,* and *Tragic Form in Shakespeare.* She has also translated into English *Selected Poems of Chaim Nachman Bialik.*

JILL MANN is Lecturer in English at the University of Cambridge. She is the author of *Chaucer and Medieval Estates Satire* and is joint editor (with Piero Boitani) of *The Cambridge Chaucer Companion.*

DONALD R. HOWARD was Professor of English at Stanford University until his death in 1987. His books include *The Idea of the* Canterbury Tales and *Writers and Pilgrims: Medieval Pilgrimage Narratives and Their Posterity* as well as two edited volumes of Chaucer's poetry.

LOY D. MARTIN is the author of *Browning's Dramatic Monologues and the Post-Romantic Subject.*

JANE CHANCE, Professor of English at Rice University, is the author of *The Genius Figure in Antiquity and the Middle Ages.*

GEOFFREY HUGHES, Professor of English at the University of the Witwatersrand, Johannesburg, has published on Medieval and Renaissance literature, and is the author of the forthcoming *Words in Time.*

H. MARSHALL LEICESTER, JR., Professor of English at the University of California at Santa Cruz, has written and published numerous articles on Chaucer, Beowulf, and the French Revolution.

MORTON W. BLOOMFIELD was Professor of English at Harvard University until his death in 1987. Among his many publications are *Essays and Explorations: Studies in Ideas, Language, and Literature*, *Linguistic Introduction to the History of English* (with Leonard Newmark), and many essays on Anglo-Saxon and Medieval literature.

PATRICIA J. EBERLE has taught at the University of Texas and at Harvard University. Currently she is Lecturer in the Department of English at the University of Toronto.

BARBARA NOLAN is Professor of English at the University of Virginia. She is the author of articles on Chaucer and Dante and *The Gothic Visionary Perspective*.

Bibliography

Andrew, Malcolm. "Chaucer's 'General Prologue' to the *Canterbury Tales.*" *Explicator* 43, no. 1 (1984): 5–6.

Baldwin, Ralph. *The Unity of the* Canterbury Tales. Copenhagen: Rosenkilde og Bagger, 1955.

Baum, Paull F. *Chaucer: A Critical Appreciation*. Durham, N.C.: Duke University Press, 1958.

Bowden, Muriel. *A Commentary on the General Prologue to the* Canterbury Tales. 2d ed. New York: Macmillan, 1967.

Brewer, D. S. *Chaucer*. 3d ed. London: Longmans, 1973.

Bronson, Bertrand H. *In Search of Chaucer*. Toronto: University of Toronto Press, 1960.

Brooks, Harold F. *Chaucer's Pilgrims: The Artistic Order of the Portraits in the Prologue*. London: Methuen, 1962.

Clawson, W. H. "The Framework of the *Canterbury Tales.*" *University of Toronto Quarterly* 20 (1951): 137–54.

Coghill, Nevill. *The Poet Chaucer*. 2d ed. London: Oxford University Press, 1967.

Cook, Albert S. "Chaucerian Papers: I." *Transactions of the Connecticut Academy of Arts and Sciences* 23 (1919): 5–10.

Cunningham, J. V. "The Literary Form of the Prologue to *The Canterbury Tales.*" *Modern Philology* 49 (1951–52): 172–81.

Curry, Walter Clyde. *Chaucer and the Medieval Sciences*. New York: Barnes & Noble, 1960.

David, Alfred. *The Strumpet Muse: Art and Morals in Chaucer's Poetry*. Bloomington: Indiana University Press, 1976.

Donaldson, E. Talbot. *Speaking of Chaucer*. Durham, N.C.: Labyrinth, 1983.

———, ed. *Chaucer's Poetry: An Anthology for the Modern Reader*. 2d ed. New York: John Wiley & Sons, 1975.

Duncan, Edgar H. "Narrator's Points of View in the Portrait-sketches, Prologue to the *Canterbury Tales.*" In *Essays in Honor of Walter Clyde Curry*, 77–101. Nashville, Tenn.: Vanderbilt University Press, 1955.

Elliott, R. W. V. *Chaucer's Prologue to the* Canterbury Tales. New York: Barnes & Noble, 1963.

Green, Eugene. "The Voices of the Pilgrims in the General Prologue to *The Canterbury Tales.*" *Style* 9 (1975): 55–81.

Higgs, Elton D. "The Old Order and the 'Newe World' in the General Prologue to the *Canterbury Tales.*" *Huntington Library Quarterly* 45 (1982): 155–73.

Hodgson, Phyllis, ed. *General Prologue to the* Canterbury Tales. London: Athlone, 1969.

Hoffman, Arthur W. "Chaucer's Prologue to Pilgrimage: The Two Voices." *ELH* 21 (1954): 1–16.

Howard, Donald R. "Chaucer the Man." *PMLA* 80 (1965): 337–43.

———. *The Idea of the* Canterbury Tales. Berkeley: University of California Press, 1976.

Hulbert, J. R. "Chaucer's Pilgrims." *PMLA* 64 (1949): 823–28.

Jordan, R. M. *Chaucer and the Shape of Creation.* Cambridge: Harvard University Press, 1967.

———. "Chaucer's Sense of Illusion: Roadside Drama Reconsidered." *Journal of English and Germanic Philology* 29 (1962): 19–33.

Kirby, Thomas A. "The General Prologue." In *Companion to Chaucer Studies,* edited by Beryl Rowland, 208–28. London: Oxford University Press, 1968.

Kittredge, George L. *Chaucer and His Poetry*. Cambridge: Harvard University Press, 1915.

Knight, S. T. " 'Almoost a Spanne Brood.' " *Neophilologus,* no. 52 (1968): 178–80.

Lawler, Traugott. *The One and the Many in the* Canterbury Tales. Hamden, Conn.: Archon, 1980.

Lawlor, John. *Chaucer.* London: Hutchinson University Library, 1968.

Lenaghan, R. T. "Chaucer's General Prologue as History and Literature." *Comparative Studies in Society and History* 12 (1970): 73–82.

Lowes, John L. *Geoffrey Chaucer.* Bloomington: Indiana University Press, 1958.

Lumiansky, R. M. "Benoit's Portraits and Chaucer's General Prologue." *Journal of English and Germanic Philology* 55 (1956): 431–38.

———. *Of Sondry Folk.* Austin: University of Texas Press, 1955.

Major, John. "The Personality of Chaucer the Pilgrim." *PMLA* 75 (1960): 160–62.

Malone, Kemp. *Chapters on Chaucer.* Baltimore: Johns Hopkins University Press, 1951.

Manly, John Matthews. *Some New Light on Chaucer.* New York: P. Smith, 1952.

Mann, Jill. *Chaucer and Medieval Estates Satire: The Literature of Social Classes and the* General Prologue *to the* Canterbury Tales. Cambridge: Cambridge University Press, 1973.

Mohl, Ruth. *The Three Estates in Medieval and Renaissance Literature.* New York: Columbia University Press, 1933.

Morgan, Gerald. "The Design of the *General Prologue* to the *Canterbury Tales.*" *English Studies* 59 (1978): 481–98.

Muscatine, Charles. *Chaucer and the French Tradition.* Berkeley: University of California Press, 1957.

Owen, Charles A., Jr. "Development of the Art of Portraiture in Chaucer's *General Prologue.*" *Leeds Studies in English,* n.s. 14 (1983): 116–33.

Pearsall, Derek. *The Canterbury Tales.* London: Allen & Unwin, 1985.

Preston, Raymond. *Chaucer.* Westport, Conn.: Greenwood, 1969.

Reidy, John. "Grouping of Pilgrims in the General Prologue to *The Canterbury Tales.*" *Papers of the Michigan Academy of Science, Arts, and Letters* 47 (1962): 595–603.

Robertson, D. W., Jr. *Chaucer's London*. New York: John Wiley & Sons, 1968.
———. *A Preface to Chaucer*. Princeton: Princeton University Press, 1962.
Robinson, F. N., ed. *The Works of Geoffrey Chaucer*. 2d ed. Boston: Houghton Mifflin, 1957.
Root, Robert K. *The Poetry of Chaucer*. Boston: Houghton Mifflin, 1922.
Ruggiers, Paul G. *The Art of the* Canterbury Tales. Madison: University of Wisconsin Press, 1965.
Schaar, Claes. *The Golden Mirror: Studies in Chaucer's Descriptive Technique and Its Literary Backgound*. Lund, Denmark: C. W. K. Gleerup, 1955.
Scheps, Walter. " 'Up Roos Oure Hoost, and Was Oure Aller Cok': Harry Bailly's Tale-Telling Competition." *Chaucer Review* 10 (1975): 113–28.
Schoeck, Richard J., and Jerome Taylor, eds. *Chaucer Criticism, Volume I:* The Canterbury Tales. Notre Dame, Ind.: University of Notre Dame Press, 1960.
Sklute, Larry. "Catalogue Form and Catalogue Style in the General Prologue of the *Canterbury Tales*." *Studia Neophilologica* 52, no. 1 (1980): 35–46.
Speirs, John. *Chaucer the Maker*. Winchester, Mass.: Faber & Faber, 1964.
Spraycar, Rudy S. "The Prologue to the 'General Prologue.' " *Neuphilologische Mitteilungen* 81 (1980): 142–49.
Swart, J. "The Construction of Chaucer's *General Prologue*." *Neophilologus* 38 (1954): 127–36.
Taylor, Paul B. "The Alchemy of Spring in Chaucer's *General Prologue*." *Chaucer Review* 17 (1982): 1–4.
Traversi, Derek. *The Canterbury Tales*. London: Bodley Head, 1983.
Tuve, Rosamond. "Spring in Chaucer and before Him." *MLN* 52 (1937): 9–16.
Wagenknecht, Edward, ed. *Chaucer: Modern Essays in Criticism*. New York: Oxford University Press, 1959.
Woolf, Rosemary. "Chaucer as a Satirist in the General Prologue to the *Canterbury Tales*." *Critical Quarterly* 1 (1959): 150–57.
Zacher, Christian. *Curiosity and Pilgrimage*. Baltimore: Johns Hopkins University Press, 1976.

Acknowledgments

"Chaucer: Motive and Mask in the General Prologue" by Ruth Nevo from *The Modern Language Review* 58, no. 1 (January 1963), © 1963 by the Modern Humanities Research Association. Reprinted by permission.

"Medieval Estates Satire and the General Prologue" (originally entitled "Conclusions") by Jill Mann from *Chaucer and the Medieval Estates Satire: The Literature of Social Classes and the General Prologue to the* Canterbury Tales by Jill Mann, © 1973 by Cambridge University Press. Reprinted by permission of Cambridge University Press.

"Memory and Form" by Donald R. Howard from *The Idea of the* Canterbury Tales by Donald R. Howard, © 1976 by the Regents of the University of California. Reprinted by permission of the University of California Press.

"History and Form in the General Prologue to the *Canterbury Tales*" by Loy D. Martin from *ELH* 45, no. 1 (Spring 1978), © 1978 by the Johns Hopkins University Press, Baltimore/London. Reprinted by permission of the Johns Hopkins University Press.

"Creation in Genesis and Nature in Chaucer's General Prologue 1–18" by Jane Chance from *Papers on Language and Literature* 14, no. 4 (Fall 1978), © 1978 by the Board of Trustees of Southern Illinois University. Reprinted by permission.

"Gold and Iron: Semantic Change and Social Change in Chaucer's Prologue" by Geoffrey Hughes from *Standpunte 137* 31, no. 5 (October 1978), © 1978 by Geoffrey Hughes. Reprinted by permission.

"The Art of Impersonation: A General Prologue to the *Canterbury Tales*" by H. Marshall Leicester, Jr., from *PMLA* 95, no. 2 (March 1980), © 1980 by the Modern Language Association of America. Reprinted by permission of the Modern Language Association of America.

"*The Canterbury Tales* as Framed Narratives" by Morton W. Bloomfield from *Leeds Studies in English* n.s. 14 (1983), © 1983 by the School of English, University of Leeds. Reprinted by permission.

"Commerical Language and the Commercial Outlook in the General Prologue" by Patricia J. Eberle from *The Chaucer Review* 18, no. 2 (1983), © 1983 by the Pennsylvania State University. Reprinted by permission of the Pennsylvania State University Press.

" 'A Poet Ther Was': Chaucer's Voices in the General Prologue to *The Canterbury Tales*" by Barbara Nolan from *PMLA* 101, no. 2 (March 1986), © 1986 by the Modern Language Association of America. Reprinted by permission of the Modern Language Association of America.

Index

VIVA Modern Critical Interpretations

Available Titles in the Series

Alice's Adventures in Wonderland

9788130906362 Rs. 145

Animal Farm

9788130906355 In Print

As You Like It

9788130918723 Rs. 195

The Adventures of Huckleberry Finn

9788130907390 Rs. 165

Beowulf

9788130907406 In Print

Beloved

9788130918884 Rs. 195

Black Boy

9788130906737 Rs. 125

Brave New World

9788130906348 In Print

Cat on a Hot Tin Roof

9788130906393 Rs. 99

VIVA Modern Critical Interpretations

Available Titles in the Series

Crime and Punishment

9788130906409 Rs. 175

The Chronicles of Narnia

9788130907468 Rs. 145

The Crucible

9788130906416 Rs. 125

Darkness at Noon

9788130906423 Rs. 145

David Copperfield

9788130918730 Rs. 145

The Death of Artemio Cruz

9788130907475 Rs. 145

Death of a Salesman

9788130906744 Rs. 125

The Divine Comedy

9788130918846 Rs. 175

Don Quixote

9788130904658 Rs. 125

VIVA Modern Critical Interpretations

Available Titles in the Series

Dracula

9788130906430 Rs. 195

Emerson's Essays

9788130906577 Rs. 175

Emma

9788130918839 Rs. 165

A Farewell to Arms

9788130918754 Rs. 175

Frankenstein

9788130907413 Rs. 145

The General Prologue to the Canterbury Tales

9788130918747 Rs. 175

The Glass Menagerie

9788130907482 In Print

The Grapes of Wrath

9788130906751 Rs. 145

Great Expectations

9788130904597 Rs. 175

VIVA Modern Critical Interpretations

Available Titles in the Series

Viva

Long Day's Journey into Night

9788130904634 Rs. 99

Lord of the Flies

9788130904603 Rs. 145

The Lord of the Rings

9788130907956 Rs. 145

The Man without Qualities

9788130907499 Rs. 145

The Merchand of Venice

9788130906522 In Print

Macbeth

97881309065[illegible]5 Rs. 125

Miss Lonelyhearts

9788130907437 Rs. 125

A Midsummer Night's Dream

9788130918914 Rs. 165

The Metamorphosis

9788130904573 Rs. 99

VIVA Modern Critical Interpretations

Available Titles in the Series

Moby-Dick

9788130906546 Rs. 165

Oedipus

9788130906768 Rs. 165

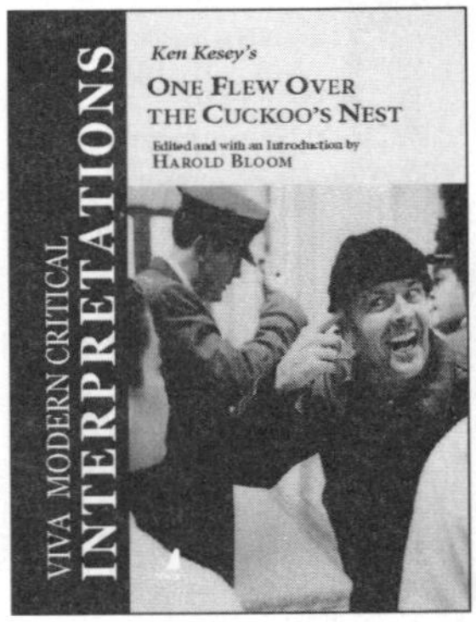

One Flew Over the Cuckoo's Nest

9788130907444 Rs. 125

One Hundred Years of Solitude

9788130907451 In Print

The Old Man and the Sea

9788130906553 Rs. 125

Othello

9788130918891 Rs. 165

Paradise Lost

9788130906560 In Print

The Pardoner's Tale

9788130904665 Rs. 125

A Passage to India

9788130906584 Rs. 145

VIVA Modern Critical Interpretations

Available Titles in the Series

Viva

Persuasion

9788130906591 Rs. 175

Pride and Prejudice

9788130906607 Rs. 195

The Red Badge of Courage

9788130906614 Rs. 145

Romeo and Juliet

9788130906621 In Print

The Rubaiyat of Omar Khayyam

9788130904641 Rs. 145

The Scarlet Letter

9788130907505 Rs. 175

Silas Marner

9788130906638 Rs. 125

Song of Solomon

9788130906645 Rs. 145

Sophie's Choice

9788130906552 Rs. 175

VIVA Modern Critical Interpretations

Available Titles in the Series

Viva

The Sound and The Fury

9788130906676 Rs. 195

A Streetcar Named Desire

9788130918716 Rs. 145

Sonnets

9788130918907 Rs. 165

A Tale of Two Cities

9788130906683 Rs. 145

The Tempest

9788130918822 Rs. 175

To Kill a Mockingbird

9788130906775 Rs. 125

Waiting for Godot

9788130906706 Rs. 99

Ulysses

9788130906690 Rs. 145

The Waste Land

9788130904689 Rs. 175

Wuthering Heights

9788130906713 Rs. 175

Young Goodman Brown

9788130906720 Rs. 125